*f*P

No Tears
in Ireland

A MEMOIR

Sylvia Couturié

THE FREE PRESS

NEW YORK   LONDON   TORONTO   SYDNEY   SINGAPORE

THE FREE PRESS
A Division of Simon & Schuster, Inc.
1230 Avenue of the Americas
New York, NY 10020

10   9   8   7   6   5   4   3   2   1

Library of Congress Cataloging-in-Publication Data

Couturié, Sylvia.
    No tears in Ireland: a memoir / Sylvia Couturié.
      p.   cm.
      1. Couturié, Sylvia. 2. Couturié, Marguerite.
3. World War, 1939–1945—Personal narratives, French.
4. French—Ireland—Biography.   I. Title.
CT868.C68 A3   2001
940.54'8144—dc21   00-063623
ISBN 0-7432-0193-0

I dedicate this book with love to my sons
JEAN-LOUIS, RICHARD and HENRI DEVIN
to my daughters-in-law
MARIE, CAROLINE and ANTONIA
and to my grandchildren
NICOLAS, ALEXIS, EMMANUEL, ANTOINE,
VICTORIA, HENRI-FRANÇOIS, ROBERT,
SOPHIE, HUBERT AND VICTOR,
also to my sister Marguerite
and for Ireland,
the land where legends remain.

Tant qu'il y aura des petites filles, l'âme de la France ne pourra mourir.

[As long as there are little girls, the soul of France cannot die.]

—Message from General de Gaulle, July 14, 1941

Contents

Foreword

TOWARD THE END of the Second World War, as the threat from German submarines receded, it was considered safe for me and my sister to take the ferry and visit our relatives in Ireland. It was the beginning of holiday years on which I still look back with nostalgia, as with swarms of cousins we made free of hospitable houses scattered over counties Waterford and Tipperary. Among the images and incidents which stud my memory—soda bread, huge teas, porridge with cream and sugar, midnight feasts, paper chases, ice-cold swims in hidden coves, mountain picnics in the rain, women in black shawls, corner boys, donkey carts—was the unexplained appearance from time to time of two young French girls, Sylvia and Marguerite, apparently without home or family. Why they were there and where they emerged from I had no idea and little curiosity either, for I was at an age when one took everything for granted, and they were only girls, after all. On our third visit to Ireland they had vanished as mysteriously as they first emerged.

My elder sister, who was of much the same age as Sylvia, remembers her more vividly than I do, as warm and attractive, and rather more sophisticated than her own schoolgirl friends. I am sure that is how she was, for the personality she describes is recognizably that of Sylvia as I know her today; and yet sophistication was not what one would have expected from the very odd setting from which she was occasionally allowed to emerge.

For Sylvia and Marguerite were in effect shipwrecked castaways, cut off from France, family and home by the outbreak of the war and marooned on—not quite a desert island, but even so a three-room beach bungalow on a strand five miles out of Dungarvan is near enough to a desert island out of season. Here they spent nearly three years without running water, proper heating or sanitation, with very little money and less education, almost no news from home, and under the control of a neurotic, possessive and jealous Irish governess, who did her best to keep them away from all outside contacts. Here they would have remained until the end of the war, if a gale and high tide, flooding the bungalow and sweeping two of its neighbors out to sea, had not led to their being rescued by the coast guard and removed to friendlier surroundings.

I learned a little of what had happened from conversations with my Irish relatives when I grew up, or with Sylvia herself when I met her in France in later years. But until I read *No Tears in Ireland* I had no idea of the full remarkable story, so vividly told, so poignant in its recreation of the loneliness of childhood, but leaving one full of admiration for the determination, humor and resourcefulness of a young girl who refused to let life get her down.

—MARK GIROUARD

No Tears
in Ireland

Château du Mesnil.

PROLOGUE

The Telegram

A COLD BREEZE was blowing into the room and stirring the curtains covering the French doors to the terrace. That was strange. I had closed them before going to bed. I dislike leaving doors open. In the distance I could hear the faint, sad music of a fiddle sounding a plaintive Irish melody.

My skin turned to gooseflesh and the hair prickled on the back of my neck. As that music wafted out of the darkness and my eyes tried to pierce the shadows, I saw the figure, standing still by the fireplace. I shivered under my sheet. The figure whispered to me, in that unmistakable brogue, "Sylvia, Sylvia Couturié, do you not recognize me?"

The face appeared out of the gray, just as I remembered it, ageless, flat and white. That face and that music coming to me out of the shadows, across time, the words, that voice, so long silent, "Sylvia, don't you recognize me?" The door slammed with a bang and she was gone. I was alone again in the dark.

Trembling uncontrollably, I sank deeper into my bed, the mists of my childhood swirling. I could see myself as I was then, a child, running up the wide steps of my parents' house, the Château du Mesnil. Running close behind me was my sister, redheaded and smaller than I. And behind her came the broad, somber figure of our Irish governess,

Miss Kathleen Walsh. The indomitable Wally. As real now across the decades as she had been then. Towering over us. Long gone and still present. I lay there, trembling.

Morning came, its pale light pushing back the darkness, with a pounding on my bedroom door. "Entrez," (come in) I called out in my sleepy voice, the voice that is mine when I have slept badly. The door flew open, and in bounded a little boy, my son, Jean-Louis. Up and onto the bed he bounced, excited, eager to read me the telegram he clutched in his small hand. I gave my permission, hesitantly, telegrams being what they are, messages of serious things. In a clear, deliberate voice, he read the solitary line: Kathleen Walsh died last night. R.I.P.

"What is R.I.P., Maman?" he asked. I took the crumpled thing and read it myself. "Requiescat in pace," I told him—rest in peace in English—as I read it over to myself, my eyes tearing up. Kathleen Walsh died last night. R.I.P. No address, no signature, just that.

"Maman, who is Kathleen Walsh? You never talked about her. Who is she? Don't cry Maman, you never cry. You have tears. Don't cry. Tell me who she is."

"Mon cheri, I promise you, one day I will tell you about her."

"Maman, please get up, come on. I just caught a great big fish, bigger than my hand. Come see." Already his mind moved on, in the way of youth. Resilient, shimmering, fleeting youth.

I got out of bed and put on my dressing gown. Without shoes, as in my adolescence, and holding my son firmly by the hand, we ran out of the house and across the lawn, the grass good against my feet. We ran across the daffodils, laughing, down to the lake, to admire the "enormous" fish caught by my proud little boy, which lay still and cold on the grass, shimmering in the sun.

The oldest part of the Château du Mesnil, built in the seventeenth century, was covered with Virginia creeper in the 1930s.

CHAPTER ONE

Le Mesnil

THE CHÂTEAU DU MESNIL was covered with ivy on one side and on the other with Virginia creeper that turned a fiery red during the last days of summer and all through the autumn. On sunny days the four tall towers were reflected in the clear waters of a small river just beyond the well-kept lawns. As a child gazing out of the French windows of the dining room, my eyes would wander over the tender green expanse, to the slow flowing river and the fields beyond. I could see the thoroughbred mares with their long-legged foals quietly grazing together with some of the best Normandy cattle in France. This was our home and we loved it. I was born there, just as my father and grandfather had been, and my family had owned it for many years.

Built in the seventeenth century and enlarged in the early part of the nineteenth, the château had a strong sense of place and a strong personality. Central heating and blazing log fires kept the rooms, with their wood paneling and painted beams, comfortably warm in winter, and armfuls of fresh flowers brightened them through spring, summer and autumn. The house was always full of people: my grandmother, my parents, our nanny, the servants and often my visiting cousins. To me the old house was alive, breathing in rhythm to the beat and musical pitter-patter of many feet.

5

In the drawing room and in the corridors hung family portraits. Among them was a fine picture of my grandmother, who had been one of the most beautiful women of her day. Many old prints of racing and hunting scenes, caricatures of hunting friends and pictures of race horses hung there as well. Some were by the Baron Karl Reille, a friend of my parents who lived in Touraine and painted hunting watercolors which he sold, to "keep his hounds well fed," or so he said.

The windows had white shutters, and these were to the house what eyelids are to people—they would open in the morning, and close again at night. In the eyes of a child, the château with its four round towers was a castle where long ago a fairy princess must have dwelled.

The landscaping around the house had been designed by Adolphe Alphand, who had created the Bois de Boulogne for Napoleon III. The large variety of trees he had planted had long since grown to rich maturity. The walled vegetable garden was always full of delicious surprises. As the sun became warmer each spring the gooseberries, raspberries and strawberries faithfully ripened to the wonder and delight of a greedy little girl.

My little sister, Marguerite, had been named after our very beautiful grandmother. Like her namesake, she also had dark red hair and green eyes. I had been christened Sylvia for no particular reason. I had not been expected to be a girl anyway, and years later, my father would sometimes tease me by saying that he had named me after the first top-class thoroughbred mare my grandfather had owned and loved.

"There is a big silver trophy in the dining-room, won at Pau by my father in 1876, and all the details to prove it," he would say. I laughed, and thought that it was much more amusing to be named after a prizewinning filly than after a saint or a grandmother.

It seemed normal for us to have ponies. Mine was called Tommy. He was a Welsh pony with a great personality and was given to me by my father for my ninth birthday.

Marguerite's gentle Shetland pony Dots had been for many years the joy of our older Decazes cousins. Dots had a sweet temperament and lived to a great age.

I was a healthy, lively, independent child and enjoyed playing pranks and tricks on grown-ups. With ever-bubbling energy and an insatiable urge for movement I always said that when I grew up I wanted to be an explorer or at least marry one, and travel the world. I loved to laugh and giggled at the slightest provocation. Not always in the best of taste, my pranks were seldom appreciated.

One day my father said to me "Your cousin François de Boislisle is arriving tonight to spend a few days here."

"How old is he, Papa?" I was excited at the idea of having a new playmate of my own age.

"He is older than you are."

"Which room will he have?"

"The blue room next to yours," my father said, seemingly already elsewhere with his thoughts as I had noticed grown-ups often were.

I had trouble going to sleep that night. Next morning at dawn I got up and went straight to the laundry room, found a large pitcher, filled it with cold water and went quietly toward my cousin's room. Inside it was dark but I could distinguish a human shape lying in the bed. I lifted the pitcher and stifling a laugh emptied its contents over the head of the sleeper.

There was a furious roar, and to my horror a tall man with a black beard and eyes blacker yet jumped out of bed. "Who are you?" he asked very crossly.

"Oh gosh, I am Sylvia," I answered, hanging my head in shame, "and you, I suppose, are my cousin François? Please forgive me, I thought you were my age. How could I know you were an old man?"

"I am not old," he protested, "I'm nineteen and at l'Ecole Navale, and you deserve a good spanking."

"Yes, I know . . . but please don't say anything to Papa or Maman."

"No, but go back to bed right away, you little devil.

Bon Dieu, de Bon Dieu de merde. What a child!" He continued to swear using interesting words I had never heard before.

Another prank that turned out badly was a bet that I made one morning with my cousin Colette Couturié, whose father was a famous polo player, that I could ride Tommy right through the house. With her loud encouragement, Tommy and I gingerly climbed the flight of steps leading to the front door, passed through the hall and were getting ready to cross the dining room over carpets and parquet when my father's voice stopped my heart.

"What the devil do you think you are doing?"

"I thought you were out," I said, "I am just having a small bet with my cousin . . ."

"Get out of here immediately," he said sternly. He was not amused. I got off my pony and led him back past the hall table out of the house and down the wide steps. Then someone took his bridle and my father caught me by the scruff of the neck and, with his riding crop, applied to my derrière the spanking of my life. Usually, when I was punished I never cried but I have to admit that on that morning my howls could be heard not only throughout the entire house but all the way to the farm and the stables. For the next few days sitting down was most uncomfortable.

I suppose I was an undisciplined, naughty child with too much energy and imagination. I was also very lonely, as there were few other children of my age to play with at Le Mesnil. Marguerite, three years younger than I and often called "Bébé," was a quiet little girl but very stubborn. She would fly into terrible tantrums when she did not get what she wanted. She would scream, throw herself on the floor, roll over and lie flat on her back. Her face would first become red, then black then white.

"She will work herself into a fit," Nanny Roberts said. During these scenes she would half swallow her tongue and grown-ups would rush to her aid, afraid that she might suffocate. On recovery, to my indignation, she was often given what she wanted. She became a spoiled child.

Grand-Maman Madame Charles Raoul-Duval, my maternal
grandmother, born in San Francisco.

I sometimes wished I could get what I wanted by employing this technique she had perfected. I tried very hard on a couple of occasions but it didn't work and my only reward was to be punished. There was nothing I could do; it was a special gift, I thought, like having a lovely voice and being able to sing.

WE HAD AN ENGLISH NANNY because it was important that we speak both French and English. Most of our circle spoke German as well. It was part of one's education. One summer evening there appeared in our nursery the most beautiful little girl I had ever seen, my cousin Myriam de Lesseps. She had thick curly blond hair, large sea-blue eyes and a shy smile. She was a little older than I. We had never met, but I was told to be kind to her and not to tease her because her father was very sick. This was not difficult, transfixed as I was by her charming manners, her lovely face and her pretty clothes. A few days later my father had to tell her that her Papa had died. She didn't cry, but her eyes became even larger and sadder and more lovely. My heart ached for her.

"Come," I said, and hand in hand we went to my secret hiding place under a large willow tree by the river. There, hidden by a curtain of green leaves, I put my arm over her shoulder to comfort her, and asked her where she lived.

"A Paris," she said, and "Aux Granges."

"Are Les Granges like Le Mesnil?" I asked.

"Bigger, with a real moat and a drawbridge, and not far from the drawbridge lives an eagle, who's tied by his foot so that he can't fly away. The house is so big that it is wonderful to play hide and seek, even to roller skate." Then her eyes filled with fear and in a low voice she said, "There are also lots of rats."

"Rats!" I said looking at her with horror.

"Oh yes," she said calmly, "and one night I was woken

up by quite a big one nibbling my finger. So I screamed and woke up Nanny."

"How horrible—what happened then?"

"Maman had my bed moved to another room and Nanny came too. Then I went back to sleep under my blanket so that the rat couldn't find me."

"Did he follow you to your new room?"

"I don't think so, but now I prefer Paris." She gave a long sigh. I was fascinated.

"Tell me about your brothers," I asked.

"Pierre and Louis? They are grown up. I seldom see them. They are too old to play with me but Papa does, or did." And her eyes again filled with tears. She remained silent for a moment, then said, "He often told me stories about my famous great grandfather Ferdinand who built the Suez Canal."

"What is the Suez Canal?" I asked.

"It's like a wide road made of water and instead of going from town to town it goes from one sea to another and ships sail up and down."

"Your great grandfather must have been very strong to do so much digging . . ." I thought of Mr. Hue, our old gardener, wearing a large straw hat and working in our walled garden.

"Oh, lots and lots of people helped him, and hundreds of camels, but great grandpapa made all the plans and the drawings." A loud bell rang three times.

"Come," I said, "lunch is ready and if we're late we'll be scolded." Together we ran back to the house.

The next day she disappeared. I longed for her to come back but she did not. After her father's funeral, she went home to be with her mother. I thought of her often and sadly also about death. So far I had only lost Judy, a Cairn terrier who had died of old age. I had cried a lot and still missed her, but losing one's Papa was much, much worse I thought, and looked at mine rather differently. The following day I asked him if he was well and when would he die. He was not amused.

LEFT: My father, Jean Charles Henri Couturié, 1884–1948.

BELOW: Me at Le Mesnil, learning to ride on my dearly loved pony, Dots.

The Couturié cousins: Marguerite, Alain, Christiane, Sylvia, Colette and Myriam de Lesseps at Le Mesnil, 1938. We lived in different parts of France but were often together during the school holidays.

Marguerite and I loved our parents very much even if we seldom saw them. I saw my father more often than my mother as I went riding with him several mornings every week, while my mother, except on the days she went hunting, usually stayed in bed in the mornings until eleven writing letters and reading the papers.

AN ENGLISH GROOM, GEORGE SMITH looked after the stables, my father's hunters and the ponies. He also taught me to ride. His wife Mabel sometimes worked in our house. They had three children, Margaret, Gladys, who was my age, and Robert. They lived in a pretty little cottage and we often played with them. My father taught me to really look and see what was around me. During these morning rides I learned the names of the trees, the birds and the crops in both French and English. Sometimes we would stop in the middle of the woods. "Listen," he would say, "what do you hear?" Sometimes it was a cuckoo or a cock pheasant, or a rabbit running over dead leaves. The loveliest mornings were those when we chanced to hear a nightingale.

"Girls," he said, "are not supposed to whistle, but I will teach you," and so he did.

I learned to recognize at a glance a field of barley, oats or wheat. In the autumn on our way home I would pick a cider apple off the tree and when I had eaten it, lean over and give Tommy the core with a friendly pat. My father was disappointed that he did not have a son and I was sorry for him. But there was nothing to be done about it except be as good a companion as I could. Not until much later did I realize how important boys were to men and women of his generation. So many men had been killed in the Great War of 1914–18, that in the France of my childhood, there was only one man left for eight women of marriageable age. The nation needed boys to repopulate and rebuild. My father talked to me gravely about the future, shaking his head.

He also told me how Le Mesnil became a stud farm. In 1906, an American friend of both my grandfathers came to France. Mr. William Astor Chanler was looking for a stud farm to buy in Normandy where he could put his thoroughbred mares for a few years because "some stupid politicians had banned all racing in America as they found betting and racing immoral."

After a few hours at Le Mesnil, when he had seen the fields, the little river, the numerous streams, the old oak trees and the horses that our family owned, he changed his mind. He asked my step-grandmother and my father—who was only a teenager at the time and whose parents had both died when he was young—"If I build stables at Le Mesnil for my mares, would you agree to look after them for me?" They both said "yes," and this partnership was a great success.

Mr. Chanler's mares stayed for several years and when their foals became racehorses, they won many French classic races. My father was very fond of Mr. Chanler and grateful for the wonderful idea that enabled him over the years, first with his stepmother and then with my mother, to turn Le Mesnil into one of the most famous stud farms in France.

"It is sad for a man not to have a son, but as you are my eldest daughter, when I die you will inherit Le Mesnil, just as I did from my father. You will have to have a sense of duty and responsibility to your sister and to the people who work on the estate, and you must promise me two things."

I would have promised him anything, so serious did he sound.

"Please don't die now, I'm only a little girl." I thought of my cousin Myriam whose father had died not long ago and who seemed so alone.

"I won't die for quite a while, don't worry, but you must promise me two things. First of all, if you can possibly avoid it, never sell any land."

"I promise," I said.

"Now promise me never to cut down any trees, and if you really have no alternative you must always replant three trees to replace the one that has fallen or that had to be cut down."

"I promise," I said again. "I hate seeing trees that are hundreds of years old being cut down. It's nearly like killing someone."

"That's true," said Papa. "There are many other ways of earning a living than by felling oaks. It is the way of greedy, lazy and stupid men."

I sometimes wondered if on these occasions my father felt that I understood, and believed that I would remember and try to do in the future as he had said. I never knew for certain, but even in my extreme youth I was well pleased that he considered it worthwhile talking to me in such a serious manner.

After these tranquil morning rides, each time learning something new, we would ride home for lunch, up the narrow lane and across the small stream. Often we whistled together and on those mornings in particular, I was very happy.

IT WAS ONLY ON SPECIAL OCCASIONS such as birthdays, Christmas and Easter that we would have our meals together with our parents. In those days in French households such as ours, the adults had their meals in the big formal dining room while the children ate with their nanny in a small dining room near the kitchen. There we learned to eat to live and not live to eat. Our meals were always very simple.

Even when they had guests, which was very often, sometimes just for meals but sometimes for weeks or months at a time, our parents ate simply. Our farms, which my father supervised directly, supplied most of the meat, and all the poultry, milk, cream and butter. The vegetable garden and orchard provided all the vegetables and fruit. The beehives in the garden were seldom silent as the bees were making honey. The forest supplied game and firewood. As the property was well over a thousand hectares, there was little need to buy much food in the shops. When there was a "good year" for wine, and my father loved good red wine, he would buy several five-hundred-liter barrels of "Pontet Canet," from a cousin who had a vineyard near Bordeaux. The barrels and bags of corks would arrive by train. The wine in the barrels then had to rest in the cellar for several months; then we waited for the moon to be the right shape in the sky. Only then was it put into bottles by our butler, Ernest Lepine, helped by his wife Marie, and everyone who was not needed for something more important. Then, carefully corked and labeled, it would age slowly in the dark cellars deep under the wide and ancient walls of Le Mesnil, waiting to be summoned into the light. The empty wine barrels were always sent back to our cousin. From special apple trees, cider and calvados were made fresh every year for ourselves and the other families working on the estate.

My father worked hard at maintaining Le Mesnil. He did not have any other significant income and always refused to hire an agent, believing that it was important to be close to the people who worked for him. He had two secretaries, Mademoiselle Chauvel, who looked after the accounts and the salaries of about forty people, and Madame Bodin, who typed his business letters and answered the telephone. They both lived in our house and usually had their meals with my parents or with us if our parents had a lot of guests.

At six every morning my father would awaken and turn on his radio, a large rectangular box on a table by his bed, from which he could hear both Paris and London. At seven he would get up, shave and dress. A little before eight he would have his breakfast, read his letters and the headlines of his newspapers, then dictate to Madame Bodin letters which he would sign in the evening. At nine-thirty he

My father and me in 1928, neither of us looking very happy at having our picture taken, and some years later setting out for our long morning ride.

would go to the stables, followed by his spaniel Smack, where George Smith would be waiting for him with Alezan, his favorite chestnut Anglo Arab. Followed by George and often by me, he would ride over some part of the estate. As the week progressed he covered all of Le Mesnil, checking on his Percheron horses, his cattle, the crops and his beloved trees. He would speak to each farmer and made a point of saying "good morning" to each farmer's wife standing by her open door or in the farmyard. He would usually inquire about her health and about her children. Everyone called him "Monsieur Jean."

Lunch was at twelve-thirty and afterwards he would return to his newspapers—*Le Figaro* for general news, both the French and English racing papers and various agricultural magazines. At two-thirty he would go to the Haras du Mesnil—the stud farm. There he would find Pierre Delangle, the stud groom, and together they would look at the mares and their foals. Some belonged to my father, others to my uncle Louis Decazes and still others to friends of my father's who were also his clients, including Lord Derby, the American Mr. Widener, and Monsieur Jean Stern.

A farm called La Chaussée, on the estate, had also been organized as a stud farm where Jacques Rivalain looked after three stallions and about thirty mares, their foals and yearlings. If it was a pleasant afternoon my mother would accompany my father in the pony trap. She loved looking at the horses and had a famously good memory for names and pedigrees. At five o'clock they came back to the house and my father would sign his letters, then retire to his favorite armchair in the drawing room, light a Camel cigarette or his pipe and drink a glass of whisky.

Every month they went to Chantilly to see the horses in training with Mr. Harry Count, the trainer. In spring, summer and autumn they frequently went to Paris for the races. On these trips they always stayed with Grandmaman, my mother's mother who was born in California and who lived in rue Raynouard. She was a great lover of racing, though less a fan of the horses than of the betting.

From October to the end of March my parents hunted roebuck twice a week. My father was on the council of Savigné l'Evêque and kept a close eye on what went on in our village, assuming as his responsibility the well-being and prosperity of all its inhabitants. This was the pattern of life at le Mesnil; it kept our parents very busy, and we did not see them often.

Each day at ten Marguerite and I would go and say "good morning" to our mother, if I wasn't already out riding. Mickey, her dachshund, slept on her bed and as a child I was frightened of him. Mickey and I didn't like each other; he always barked at us, and once he even tried to nip my ankle and I gave him a good kick. We never stayed long with our mother, as we never were quite sure whether or not we were bothering her. At eleven the cook came to tell her what she had received from the farms and the garden and suggested a menu for meals. My mother would tell her how many guests were expected.

The city of Le Mans is 12 kilometers south of Le Mesnil and shopping there with our mother was as exciting for my sister and me as it was rare. We didn't go there more than three or four times a year. Our nanny would always come with us and Maman would often look very bored. She would always insist on buying clothes two sizes too large for us so that we wouldn't grow out of them too fast. We would come home happily laden with new coats, raincoats and shoes. All of our other clothes were either home-made by Madame Rivalain, the wife of our stud groom, or inherited from our cousins and various daughters of our parents' friends. For years I wore very pretty summer dresses inherited from a mysterious Susan Diggle who lived in Yorkshire and whom I had never met.

If we went shopping in December we might visit a toy shop and afterwards go to a patisserie to eat cakes and ice cream. We never went into any other shops, were unaware they existed and were never given any pocket money.

Purchases such as meat, groceries and bread were made by the cook in the village shops of Savigné l'Evêque.

Sometimes we went to church there on Sunday morning with our nanny; or we might go to Le Mans with our mother because Mass there was said more quickly. Papa only went to funerals and family weddings.

We seldom left Le Mesnil, and that small patch of France was our childhood universe.

W HEN MARGUERITE WAS SEVEN YEARS OLD, a new governess arrived from Ireland to look after her. She was to replace Nanny Roberts, our darling old English Protestant, easygoing nanny, who wanted to retire. Her name was Miss Walsh but she immediately asked our parents and us to call her Wally. While this appeared to be a friendly gesture, it later became evident to me that it was an informality that disguised her true personality. Of medium height, her figure was heavy and flat with no soft curves, bosom, or waist. She looked like a domino on short legs. Her brown or green tweed skirt was always worn with a knitted sweater of matching color. She wore a white collar, heavy leather shoes, and a brown leather belt. Her graying brown hair was pulled back from a low brow and tied in a tight bun. Except for whitish powder (to take away the shine), she wore no makeup. Her face looked ageless and her sweet smile was a puzzling contrast to the cold pale eyes lurking behind thick wire-rimmed glasses. Her teeth were as brown as her tweeds.

Her fiancé had been killed during the 1914–18 war and that was why she had never married, she told us. A staunch Irish Catholic, her vision of humanity was narrow and generally unkind except toward the Grand Irish Catholic Church and for herself. She had The Faith—and the certainty that she would go to Heaven. To me this attitude came as a shock. I had learned simple prayers that my sister and I said kneeling by our beds every evening and we were taken to Mass fairly regularly on Sunday mornings, but there was no drama if we missed. It had been part of life like lunch or supper, and not what now seemed a daily concern with God watching us all the time. Wally spoke often of the Devil, Sin and Hell and tried to frighten me with strange stories.

Worried, I told my father about it during one morning's ride. He only laughed and said not to worry about a lot of silly nonsense, but somehow it was not that easy. With the faultless intuition of children we both distrusted Wally. We knew, Marguerite and I, that she was not sincere. I never felt she liked me, let alone ever loved me or any other child. For her we were a job, no more, no less. Our previous nannies had always come from the homes of friends or cousins. Wally came from an agency.

I suppose her job was not an easy one. It seldom was for the children's "governess" in a large household. But she made things worse by her superior attitude, giving too many orders to Solange, the little maid who looked after our rooms, ringing for her during her meal time, seldom saying "thank you" and never looking pleased. Not used to this kind of treatment, the older servants were indignant, and I noticed the difference. Maria the cook stopped slipping us extra goodies. Wally was also a snob, something that was new to me, and in consequence she kept to herself and made no friends. My mother had been told by the agency that her qualifications were suitable for taking charge of a seven-year-old, but not for older children. Busy with her friends and newspapers, her letters and her racing, hunting and social life, my mother had not taken the trouble to find out much more or to keep an eye on the new nanny's work.

Wally herself did not have the smallest doubt about her superior qualifications both in Catholic religious instruction and child education. Her job was to look after Marguerite and teach her how to read and write. I had private tutoring and liked the lessons given to me every evening by Mademoiselle Marthe, the village school teacher in Savigné l'Evêque. I did not attend school in the village for simple reasons: a lot of the village girls had lice in their hair and the local Sarthois accent was judged very unpleasant. Wally was supposed to teach me how to read and write in English, but she never did and no one noticed.

The one time I ventured to ask Wally about her family, she gave me a florid description that remained in my mind for many years. "Walsh" she said, "is an ancient Irish name. There was a king of Ireland called Walsh. I come from what is known in Ireland as landed gentry. I was born in a large house with a beautiful view of the mountains"— Le Mesnil had no view and no mountains—"Unfortunately, my father lost all his money during a revolution and that is why I have to work looking after you. I was very well educated by the nuns in Dungarvan. My fiancé was killed during the Great War and my sister Madge is married to an English officer." She stopped and lit a cigarette. It was a pity, I thought, that the holy nuns of Ireland had not taught Wally more French. Her accent was atrocious and her vocabulary extremely limited, a condition that being in France did not seem to help. I thought that it must be difficult for her coming from such a grand Irish family to mix with the less grand people of Le Mesnil. Although she was invited, at first, she never went and sat as Nanny Roberts used to do in the sewing room with the other women who worked in the house. I considered it a great treat to be invited into this "women's room," where if I was a good child I was allowed to sit on Mabel Smith's comfortable lap once she had put away her work. Maria, the cook, had her favorite armchair in which no one else dared sit and the always-smiling Solange would run down to the kitchen for hot coffee or chocolate when the day's work was over. It was a place for gentle evening conversations in one of the old round towers of the château. Wally did not care for it.

Wally smoked a great many cigarettes. She smoked in her own room and she smoked in the nursery. I asked her why. "It's my only comfort," she would say, "And it's good for my nerves." I didn't think much of it at first because my father also smoked. My mother, however, did not, and after a while I realized that Wally was being very careful to hide this habit from them. She never smoked at the time of the day they might come and see us. If they had been out and came back unexpectedly she would rush to open a window and her ashtray would disappear. I was surprised to discover that she was hiding something from my parents. I didn't tell them about it but disliked by my silence being an accomplice and couldn't help but think that she was doing something wrong if it had to be a secret. It didn't help me to like her any better.

One thing that really seemed to annoy Wally was that my father did not have a title. I didn't know much about such things so I decided to ask my cousin Rose de Bellet, who was several years older than I and lived in the village with her parents, to explain.

"Does your Papa have a title?" I asked her one day.

"Yes," she answered, "he's a Baron. Why do you ask?"

"Because Wally keeps talking about things like that and I would like to know more about them."

"Well," said Rose, "my Papa's ancestor was made a Baron centuries ago when he went on a crusade to the Holy Land with St. Louis, the King of France."

"Goody," I thought, "Wally is going to be pleased—a King and a Saint all in one."

"Does your father, like Wally, think that it's terribly important to have a title?" "Well, yes, I suppose, but he always says that what's really important is to be a gentleman."

"Is Papa a gentleman?"

"Certainly, what a silly question."

Later I told Wally about Uncle François and about King Louis of France who was also a saint. "He is only a baron," she said and she was not impressed. She continued to be annoyed that my father was "only a gentleman."

Eventually I left Le Mesnil for a boarding school called Jalesnes, recommended to my parents by their friends the Marquis and Marquise de Contades-Gizeux who had three daughters studying happily there. I was not sorry to go, and

Wally was not sorry either. But little Marguerite seemed very sad.

THE CONVENT SCHOOL OF JALESNES was about 100 kilometers south of Le Mesnil and I went there at the end of the Easter holidays in 1938. My parents decided to send me two days before the arrival of the other students to give me a chance to get acquainted with the place. It was a mistake, the sort of error most parents make out of kindness, particularly with firstborn children.

During two endless days I wandered alone through the large school buildings, empty and silent. At night I went to sleep by myself in an enormous dormitory thinking about Le Mesnil, my pony and my little sister.

On the second afternoon, more lonely and miserable than I had ever been before, I went into the nearby forest. The moldy smell made me feel better, and the mint and wild thyme calmed me with the memories of my morning rides at home. I climbed to the top of an ancient oak, sat on a branch and cried. The wise old tree held me in its arms and eventually my sobbing ceased. A little red squirrel appeared to keep me company. "Don't be sad," he seemed to say, "I am your friend," then scurried off as quickly as he had come. On the way back to the school I picked lilies of the valley and my mood lifted.

The other girls arrived the next day and screwing up my courage, I dried my tears. I had previously met the three sisters, Guyonne, Alix and Renée de Contades-Gizeux, whose parents had recommended Jalesnes but the rest were all new faces, most of them friendly. With the excitement of new schoolbooks and the discovery of large classrooms, I didn't have time to think about my pony, or my family. In fact, for the first time in my life, I was never lonely.

Situated in the Maine et Loire, a few kilometers north of the town of Saumur, the convent school was a vast château that had been the home of the Prince de Jalesnes. A dry moat surrounded the building and beyond it were many hectares of dense forest. Some girls said that not many years ago there were still wolves prowling in the area, but it was unlikely that any remained. Those who lived on nearby estates and were familiar with the region added that there were many stags and roebucks in the woods, as well as wild boars which could be very dangerous during the mating season or if wounded by a hunter.

The nuns who ran the school maintained strict discipline. All girls, including the ten-year-olds, had to wear thick black stockings. These were uncomfortably warm during the summer months. A lighter uniform was provided for the summer term, but the horrid black stockings were worn the entire year through.

Hot water was available once a day and the students had only one bath a month. Each day we washed our faces in metal basins and our bottoms in bidets. On my mother's insistence I was allowed to have a bath every week. I was the only exception. The nuns made us take our baths without removing our undershirts because nakedness was a sin. I wondered why smelly girlish bodies could be in any way more saintly than clean ones.

In June 1938 four other girls and I made our first communion. In preparation for the sacrament we made a three-day retreat, during which time we were not allowed to talk to any of the other girls and were excused from normal classes. These days were spent in prayer led by a priest who explained to us what an important event in our lives our first communion was and how much Jesus and Mary loved us.

The day before our communion we went to confession, being told to be extra careful that absolutely no sins were forgotten. We fretted over it, fearing terrible retribution if one slipped our minds or was unknown to us. In my missal I had noticed a sin that the priest never talked about and I had several times wondered why. This mysterious sin was called adultery and I added it to my list. "After all," I said to myself, "it's better to be safe than sorry, and perhaps I've committed adultery accidentally."

Into the dark confessional I went, piously knelt, and in a hushed voice whispered "Father, I have sinned. I am greedy, I love sweets and cakes, I have talked in the dormitory, I have been lazy, I have not paid attention to my teachers in class, I have made wicked faces at the nuns behind their backs and also, Father, I have committed adultery." I said this bravely, in a low voice, carefully watching the priest's face. He sat up with a jerk and coughed for what seemed a long time. Then he looked at me, a fair-haired blue-eyed little girl. "No, my child, you have not committed adultery and you must not talk about things you know nothing about. I give you absolution and for your penance you will say the rosary. Then, after practicing the procession for tomorrow's ceremony, you will help Soeur Bernadette decorate the high altar. I bless you," he said, "In the name of the Father, the Son, and the Holy Ghost." "Amen," we said together.

A little annoyed that he had sidestepped what seemed to me an interesting sin, I recited my rosary unenlightened. It was now time for rehearsing the procession of the five of us girls in long white dresses with white socks and shoes and white veils on our heads. I was the smallest and youngest, and was to walk in front, with the others following in pairs.

In the chapel on the left of the high altar were several rows of chairs and kneelers—*prie Dieu*—reserved for our parents. The whole school would be present for the High Mass which would last several hours.

We started to fast immediately after seven o'clock dinner. Not even a mouthful of water could be swallowed until after the long ceremony the following day. The rehearsal was easy: it was important to walk with our backs very straight but with our heads reverently bent, hands together holding tall white candles, careful not to trip over the unusually long skirts or walk too fast; and careful not to giggle.

Soeur Bernadette was responsible for the decoration of the chapel. She had been told by the priest that he would send a girl to help her, and she was already in the sacristy arranging flowers in the vases when I arrived. She needed me to climb up on to the altar and place vases on the high shelves so that the Blessed Sacrament would be surrounded with flowers. "Take off your shoes," she ordered. "Hurry up now, we don't have much time."

After three days of praying, I was delighted to move and do something useful. My shoes flew off and I placed a chair at the top of the three steps, then feeling rather sacrilegious, climbed up on to the altar. Soeur Bernadette passed me a heavy vase full of white lilies, roses and lilacs. I rearranged the flowers a little, deeply inhaling their intoxicating scent.

"Put it well to the left of where Monsieur l'Aumonier will place the Blessed Sacrament, that's it," the little nun said, "just there. Be still now, I'll get the second vase."

"Put this one on the other side," she ordered. When this was done, Soeur Bernadette stepped back to get a good view of her arrangement. "That's beautiful—quite beautiful, dear Lord," and she murmured to herself a silent prayer. Then forgetting where I was standing, I stepped back also to judge for myself the great beauty of the scene. In doing so, with a scream of terror and with arms and legs waving I tumbled off the altar onto my head.

The next morning I was the disgrace of the school, as in front of parents and visitors I led the procession of good little girls down the aisle to Holy Communion with a scratched face and a black eye. I remember my mother's astonished face, her round eyes and open mouth.

Me looking very serious for the photo of my first passport in 1939.

CHAPTER TWO

Holiday

*E*NGLAND WAS A COUNTRY my parents knew well, having partly been educated there. It was a land they loved and where they had many friends. Years later I discovered that my mother had an aunt and two English cousins who lived in Somerset and that my father had an English godfather.

Every year they went to England, to hunt or shoot and compare various agricultural and racing interests with their friends. For both business and pleasure they went to Ascot, Epsom, Goodwood or Newmarket race meetings. Last but not least, Papa had to go to London to see his tailor.

Their English friends loved coming to France in their turn and would stay at Le Mesnil for happy weeks. I remember Bunty and Petsy Scrope who always came for the twenty-four-hour motor car race at Le Mans, and wartime friends of my father, the Diggles and Jan de Cabrol. And of course everyone came to see the horses.

There were many others whose names I have forgotten, but not the visits of famous old Lord Derby, who was very fat. He once got stuck in his bath and had to be pulled out by four people in a damp mix of embarrassment and laughter. Many also came to Deauville in August, for the annual yearling sales, including an American contingent, all of whom then continued on to Paris where their wives would buy their clothes.

Although it was their habit to travel to England, my

parents decided in 1938 to alter their annual routine to include Ireland. There were several reasons for the change. First of all, sport: Papa loved to fish. Secondly, there were sentimental reasons. Maman's mother, a Californian, was a Tobin of Irish descent. Lastly, given our new Irish governess it now seemed that the time was right. In a natural combination of business and pleasure, my parents looked forward to visiting the famous Irish stud farms, home of many great horses, and afterwards to salmon and trout fishing in the rivers and lakes of western Ireland.

It would be good for the girls, they said, to spend the summer there, particularly for Sylvia to improve her English. At my French boarding school I was either forgetting how to speak English or pretending that I had forgotten, not wishing to be different from my new friends. I liked the feeling of belonging and thought speaking a second language would set me apart. As with many children, I had no desire to stand out. It made me insecure. If you are different, you are left alone and I did not want to be alone. I wanted to fit in.

As carefully as it was planned, this exciting holiday of summer 1938, it fell apart as quickly. One day my mother had a high temperature, the next she was seriously ill. "Hepatitis" declared Dr. Poussin, the village doctor. "Stay in bed and rest, eat lightly and no traveling." As simply as that, plans for an Irish holiday were set aside until the following year.

Instead while our parents were in Deauville, Wally, Marguerite and I went to stay in a small hotel in Locquirec, Brittany. Day after day, throughout the month of August, the sun shone with uninterrupted brilliance and warmth. Our world was reduced to a sandy beach and a calm blue sea. I learned to swim, and with scores of other children to play with, I was happy.

In fact, 1938 lives in my memory as an idyll, even if odd scraps of adult conversation penetrated our happy summer frolicking on the beaches with other French children. We learned of a German politician called Hitler who made a lot of noise on the radio and boasted of possessing a great army. We learned he had an Italian friend whose name was Mussolini. The words *Führer* and Dictator were often heard, but their meaning was less clear to us, and unmenacing in the sun. Cities such as Berlin and Rome, formerly only names in geography lessons, became places where people lived, worked and died.

Marguerite and I, intrigued by fragments of serious conversations, decided to call our pet tortoises Hitler and Mussolini. Unlike their namesakes they never became celebrities, and as tortoises have very long lives they are perhaps eating tender lettuce leaves to this day in a quiet and lovely high-walled garden of the Sarthe.

In September Marguerite started her lessons again, with Wally puffing away on her cigarette. Neither of them enjoyed it. Marguerite did not like Wally's ceaseless reminders of how hardworking her previous charges, the Horgan children, had been, and how lazy she was. I told Marguerite not to mind. After one more year, she would be able to go to boarding school with me.

I returned to Jalesnes where, for the first time in my life, I studied seriously. I had no choice. Although my parents received fine educations themselves, they never paid much attention to ours. I only learned how to read French fluently at the age of nine, and although we both spoke English, we had no idea how to read or write it. My mother had tried halfheartedly to teach me to read English, with the help of the Beatrix Potter "Peter Rabbit" books, but I had found them dull and babyish. After a short time and to my relief, they were put aside and forgotten.

I was a proud little girl and I was secretly ashamed of the low grades I had obtained the previous term. I knew that I could do better by working hard. There was keen competition at Jalesnes, and in general the girls were both diligent and intelligent. I welcomed the new subjects, algebra and Latin, because with these I did not start with the same handicap I had with French and arithmetic. Most of the teachers were kind and, as I was small for my age, I was

A formal portrait of Marguerite and me, taken to be sent to family in 1938.

Château de Gizeux, the ancestral home of the Marquis de Contades-Gizeux in Touraine.

allowed to sit in the front row of the class. I was interested in everything, always eager and happy to learn.

*T*HAT WINTER, DURING A BREAK FROM SCHOOL, I had two particularly exciting days out hunting on Tommy, my pony. The traditional pageantry of the French hunting scene, with its origins dating back to medieval times, was a part of life at Le Mesnil and is one of the most vivid and cherished memories of my childhood.

The hunts we took part in were hosted at Gizeux, a vast, sandy and Pinacea-fir-wooded estate, by the Marquis de Contades-Gizeux. The beautiful château, standing proudly halfway up a hill, was framed by tall trees. Below it a small river flowed through a valley dotted with lakes. Many years before, in the same Loire Valley, it was the Château d'Ussé that inspired Perrault to write his timeless fairy tale *Sleeping Beauty*. Only a few kilometers away, the Château de Gizeux shared that magical atmosphere.

I was always in a state of suppressed excitement as the hour of the hunt—or more precisely "the meet"—drew near. At five minutes to eleven at the left of the stately court-yard, one could see the hunt servants waiting, some holding the bridles of their masters' horses, the others keeping the impatient hounds together *en meute*—in pack.

Nearer the château I could see our hosts and their children greeting their guests, men and women dressed in traditional French hunting clothes. Designed in the days of Louis XV, they are markedly different from those worn in England and the United States. In France each pack, or *équipage*, has its own colors and its own buttons. The shiny buttons are made out of brass or silver, sometimes both, and are engraved with the design of either the head or the whole animal hunted by that particular équipage. The clothes are tailored from solid warm cloth and with velvet cuffs and collars. The colors range across the spectrum, each more gorgeous than the last, in ever more vibrant combinations, no two "Hunts" being identical.

One of my favorites was a particular shade of beige known as *ventre de biche,* which in English means the color of a doe's belly. My father had told me this *tenue d'équipage* (particular outfit) had originally belonged to the Prince de Condé. A few days before the old Prince died, he asked his friend, the Baron de Champchevrier who had hunted with him for many years to come and see him.

"My friend," he said, "I know that my days on this earth are numbered. You can give me one of my last great pleasures by accepting for yourself, your family and friends my traditional hunting clothes, colors and buttons."

The Baron accepted, and both old men had tears in their eyes as they bid each other Adieu. To this day, the descendants of Baron de Champchevrier can be seen hunting stag and roebuck over a large part of Touraine wearing the *tenue d'équipage* of the Prince of Condé.

On a carefree February morning in 1939, I watched the crowd grow in the courtyard. The village people and the local farmers came on foot or on bicycles. The bell of the little church chimed eleven o'clock. The Marquis de Contades-Gizeux and his *piqueur* (huntsman) mounted their horses. It was the signal for the others to do the same. Slowly, with the hounds behind them, they rode together across the drawbridge.

The master and his huntsman then gracefully and solemnly lifted their shining French hunting horns from their shoulders, and raised them to their lips. First the Marquis de Contades-Gizeux, then the huntsman and then together they rang out the joyful notes of a traditional fanfare. The lively music rose high and far in the cold winter sky. The first tune, called "the departure for the hunt," was the first of many horn calls that would be heard over the course of the day, carrying messages in the secret voices of the ancient language of French forests.

The colorful group was setting out to spend that cold,

bright day hunting roebuck, a small deer that is the wildest of all the wild animals of the forest. Never has a roebuck been circus trained. Wild boars and stags are both brave and strong, but rely entirely on their physical might to out-run the hounds. They nearly always run either in a straight line or in certain predictable directions, often against the wind, letting it carry back to the hounds the precious scent. The roebuck is more intelligent, more cunning and more gifted by nature to defend himself. Like the hare, he goes with the wind, making the task much more difficult for the hounds. His scent is light, and the longer he runs and the more tired he gets, the lighter it becomes. He will walk for kilometers up and down in a small stream where no one will be able to find his hoof marks. When he gets tired, he will seek out other roebucks in the vicinity to get them to run for a while in his place. As they look much alike, it makes the pursuit very difficult for both hunters and hounds. Often, after several hours of good sport, galloping over fields and through forests, jumping many ditches and crossing streams, there is no kill. If the roebuck finds a good hiding place, in a ditch, under a fallen tree or in a pile of wood, there is no scent and he is not found. This is a great frustration for the hounds who have worked hard all day, but they will be given some good hot soup on their return to the kennels. I always disliked seeing an animal killed, even when I knew that the hounds deserved a reward. As this did not happen every time, and when it did it was very quick, I loved hunting the gallant roebuck.

I would also have my private game on hunting days. This consisted of pushing Tommy as fast as he would go, through thick undergrowth and over ditches, to escape from the grown-ups, and get closer to the hounds.

Twice, my mother came to Jalesnes for me so I could join the hunt. The nuns always refused to allow me to put on my jodhpurs before I left, saying that it was not right for girls to wear trousers. I would leave the school in my uni-form, but Charles the chauffeur would stop the car near a small wood. There I would disappear behind a tree, and replace my uniform and my thick black stockings with a polo neck sweater, jodhpurs, a tweed jacket and a riding cap.

My father always looked very smart, and so did my pretty mother riding sidesaddle on a gray mare. They hunted regularly on Tuesdays and Saturdays from early October to the end of March. Afterwards there was always a large party. Everyone brought food and wine and would sit at long candle-lit tables well into the night reliving that day's hunt and those of days past.

We took for granted those days of peace. No one knew how few of them were left to us. I do however remember a portent outside of our carefree hunting circle. Late one night in June, all the girls and the nuns watched a beautiful aurora borealis from the school dormitory windows. The awed silence was broken by the gloomy voice of an old nun.

"An aurora borealis in France means war in the near future." I was not the only one to be frightened as I went to my dormitory bed that night.

*A*S SUMMER DREW NEARER and plans for our Irish holiday became more precise, my excitement grew. Wally, Marguerite and I were to go ahead, and our parents would join us in September after the Deauville season. They always stayed at the Hotel Royal, went racing nearly every day, and faced the ordeal of having to sell their thoroughbred yearlings in that most demanding of markets. These sales were of utmost importance to them because they represented the major part of the income of the stud farm— Haras du Mesnil. Horses could be great fun, but they were also a serious business. Most people had children, and they were taken pretty much for granted. But racehorses were exceptional, especially good ones, and they invariably had the good taste never to argue or ask questions. They took up more of our parents' time than we did, or so it seemed to me.

Jacques-Henri de Durfort and me with our ponies getting ready to
follow a hunt at Le Lude in 1939.

My mother with Tahiti after she won the Prix de Diane in 1954, ridden
by Maurice Larraun in our family racing colors.

For us it was to be a bungalow by the sea rented from Mr. Horgan, the solicitor for whom Wally had worked for several years before coming to France, looking after his two children, David and Joan.

We left Le Mesnil at dawn on a cool end-of-July morning in 1939. Charles, an easy, kindhearted man, patient with children, drove us to Le Havre. We traveled on an enormous transatlantic passenger ship that was en route to New York via Southampton and Cork. Marguerite and I escaped from Wally and went exploring on the different decks. We were fascinated by the lifeboats and by the pure scent of the open sea, far out from land. The passageways were narrow, the stairways steep, and below deck the cabins were warm with a slight strange smell coming from the ship's engines that was quite different from the usual odors in a house or hotel. After supper we went to bed in a cabin that had three bunk beds. Wally took the one on the inside of the cabin and I climbed to the upper bunk above Marguerite. I wanted to be able to look out of the open porthole.

Too excited to sleep, I was also in pain—a big molar was growing in. Suddenly, in the middle of the night, the sky lit up. Thinking that it was the rising sun, I stared out of the porthole. But it wasn't the sun. Strange things were happening. In the far distance was a vast fire. The sea itself seemed to be burning. For a long time I watched, until mystified and frightened I finally retreated under the blankets. Unable to sleep, I repeated to myself in a low voice: "Water doesn't burn! I don't understand, water doesn't burn!" Years later, I learned that pouring oil on the surface of the sea and setting it alight was part of a British naval war exercise.

M R. AND MRS. HORGAN met us when we got off the ship at Cork and took us to spend the night at their home called Lacaduv on the outskirts of the city. To my embarrassment, as we got out of the car my sister asked, "Why do you live in such a little house, Mr. Horgan?"

There Marguerite and I met David and Joan, about whom we had heard so much from Wally. They were a few years older than we, very tall and skinny. When we were out of earshot of the grown-ups, Marguerite asked them if they had always been as good and studious as Wally said. Joan had a keen sense of humor and her eyes shone behind her spectacles as she giggled.

"No, no, Wally did exactly the same thing to us. She was always saying that we were unbearable, horrible, and that the children she had been with before had been perfect angels."

"Well, that answers a thing or two. I had always wondered," said Marguerite with a note of relief in her baby voice. We all became friends.

The next day, under heavy rain, Mr. Horgan drove us down the "wrong" side of the road to his bungalow near Crosshaven. It stood alone, high on a cliff with a wonderful view of the sea. We settled ourselves comfortably and Wally, who could now smoke in peace, found a young girl to do the housework. Maureen O'Sullivan was a tall Celtic beauty with blue eyes and black hair who claimed to live on tea, dancing and fresh air. Clearly she thrived on it.

The village she returned to each evening could not boast of a hall of any sort, only an area in the open air in the middle of which stood a dance floor. In consequence, rain precluded dancing. One evening, invited by Maureen, we persuaded Wally to take us down to watch. Electric bulbs were strung over the area and a blind man with an accordion provided what was needed in the way of lively music. For the first time in our lives we heard the lovely Irish melodies. From the very first notes we were captivated. We thought it magical. The three of us sat for a whole hour on a damp wooden bench watching the colleens dance with the Irish boys, keeping an affectionate eye on "our Maureen."

"I want to learn how to dance like that before August is over," I said, tapping my feet to the rhythm.

"Me too," said Marguerite.

"You always keep saying 'Me too.' Try and have some ideas of your own. After all, you're now eight." She stuck out her tongue at me.

"You're a baby, you're still a baby, baby Marguerite," I chanted.

Wally, who had not been, to say the least, enthusiastic about the evening's entertainment, had had enough. To my astonishment she slapped our faces hard for the first time. I was speechless as she hurried us home saying she would never take us to watch the dancing again. Wally did not approve of dancing.

*I*N CONTRAST TO THE BRILLIANT SUNSHINE and the crowds of children we had enjoyed playing with during the previous summer holiday on the Brittany coast, the skies here remained continually overcast. Day after day we were confined to the house, with the choice of sitting by the window leafing through last year's newspapers and magazines, which we couldn't read, or looking out at the Atlantic Ocean disappearing into driving rain or gray mist. This came as a bitter disappointment to us after looking forward so much to these summer holidays in a foreign country. We found ourselves hoping that the month would soon be over and that our parents would arrive. Wally would then leave on her own holiday and as a family we would visit the beautiful lakes and streams of western Ireland. As once we had yearned for August, now we yearned for September—and the sooner the better.

That September, however, childhood came to a sudden end for many young Europeans. Happy teenage years would never be. I remember with perfect clarity Sunday the third of September, 1939. Even then I realized that things would never be the same, that terrible events loomed. Wally was panic-stricken when we heard on the wireless that the war had started. "What am I going to do?" she wailed. "A woman alone with two brats on my hands and no more money." Then she cried, "Your parents said that they were coming and now obviously they can't. For all as I know, they may be dead. It's all very unfair to me."

Poor little Marguerite, sitting in a big armchair chewing her handkerchief, began to weep quietly. With her hair over her face in disarray she looked like a lost little animal, but at the same time she was fragile and lovely in her smocked dress printed with pale green flowers. She was eight years old and Wally had shocked and frightened her. I saw her tremble. Wally, lost in her personal recriminations, did not notice the weeping child.

I too was frightened and bewildered. I heard the news on the radio but could not entirely grasp what it meant. In spite of the rain, I felt compelled to escape the house and the suffocating sense of doom mercilessly fanned by Wally's melodramatics. I sought the solitude of the beach and tried to think of a solution to our immediate problem.

"One thing is certain," I said to myself. "In life, the only thing that really counts is personal capacity—the will to work, to study; the heart to love; the courage to fight. All the rest is of no importance, all the rest can disappear without a moment's notice."

Walking in a blue bathing suit on a windy Irish beach, thinking profound thoughts for an eleven-year-old, I felt myself being kicked out of childhood and into an uncertain future. I had a younger sister to console and look after, and no money. A few summer clothes were all my worldly possessions. I did not cry, but I was colder than I had ever been, cold to the marrow of my bones.

I returned to the bungalow. "Wally, we have to telephone to Mr. and Mrs. Horgan. Perhaps they'll let us stay here a little longer. And we can ask Mr. Horgan to try to find a way to contact my father. There's no reason to believe that our parents have been killed on the first day of the war," I added with a smile for my sister.

Wally thought this over for a moment and agreed. "Yes, I'll go to the village and telephone Mr. Horgan and ask him if we can stay on. You can start writing a letter to him immediately to thank him for his kindness because it's very wrong to impose on people." With new, questioning eyes I returned her gaze, but decided to let her bizarre logic go unquestioned.

Mr. and Mrs. Horgan found an intelligent solution for Wally and for us. They brought us back to their house, and Mr. Horgan telephoned Reverend Mother Superior Aloysius of the Ursuline convent school in Waterford, which his daughter Joan was attending. The Reverend Mother said that she had room for us but would only accept us if Mr. Horgan was certain that the school fees would be paid, because there was no reason why her convent should have to help two aliens.

This was a new word for me. I didn't know what it meant, but Mr. Horgan did. He was furious with the reverend mother and told her that if necessary, he would pay for the school term himself and that, to begin with, he'd send money to buy books and uniforms. In a severe voice he ended by telling the reverend mother that he was sending us to school the next day.

"Excuse me, Mr. Horgan," I asked, "What does it mean, aliens?" Still furious, he did not answer.

"Please, Mr. Horgan," I said, my face white as a sheet, "I am only a little girl—I'm only eleven. It's better that I should know right away. 'Alien'—is it another word for 'orphan'?"

Startled, Mr. Horgan looked at me kindly: "No," he said gently, " 'alien' only means foreigner." Although I didn't understand completely the meaning of that word either, it did not seem quite as bad.

The following day Wally took us by train to Waterford, and that is how Marguerite and I found ourselves behind the gray walls of an Irish convent at the beginning of the September term in 1939. As we were now boarders at the school, Mr. Horgan told Wally that she had better begin her holidays and go to stay with her sister for a while. Although she was a member of a large family of eight sisters and three brothers, this sister was the only one with whom she spoke. Her name was Madge and she was married to an English officer.

THE IRISH BOARDING SCHOOL was very different from the French one. The large gray granite building resembled a barrack block. It had always been a school, and its classrooms and refectory were immense and impersonal. Other than a sad, irregularly shaped flowerbed in front of the main entrance, its courtyards and playgrounds were barren and cheerless. The two tennis courts and the sports field were the only places I found attractive, partly because of the reassuring presence of several oak trees. The high walls surrounding the convent made me think of a prison. From within it was impossible to see the street or the small town. Unlike the other girls, our names were not sewed onto our clothes, only a number. Mine was 52. Names sewn in cost money. We had none.

The Irish girls spent much less time in the classroom and much more out on the playing fields than we did in France, and soon I too loved playing cricket and field hockey. I would chase the hockey ball for hours, enjoying myself and laughing with the other girls. On the whole they were friendly and rather curious about "the foreigners." Our strange names alone set us apart. Their names, later to fill my autograph book, were Frances Kallahan, Mary Atkinson, Pat Dooley, Deidre O'Kelly, Eileen McDermott, Pauline O'Brien from Ballyroe and Anne Walsh.

In class, I was often either desperately worried or in a total daze and looking out of the window at the passing clouds. I had already experienced trouble with arithmetic and now I was bottom of the class again, learning a totally new way of counting. To find the correct answer to the sum of eleven pence halfpenny plus seven pence farthing presented an almost insurmountable problem. Even worse was the fact that at the age of eleven, I could only barely read English and was quite unable to write it. French, of course, was no longer part of the menu for me, being reserved for the older girls.

Luckily for me, there was an old Belgian nun in the convent, Mother Agnes. Large and round, with an open, pleasant face, her kind brown eyes watched from beneath heavy straight brows. Her coif, veil and her starched plastron set off the rosiness of her cheeks. She knew what homesickness meant, and understood and shared my anxiety. Her entire family was in Belgium. She was one of the older nuns and the school's French teacher. She lent me many books in both languages, helped both Marguerite and me keep up our native tongue, and taught me to read English. I remember in particular working our way through *Oliver Twist*.

"It is important for you to know," she said, "that there have always been, and unfortunately always will be, very poor children in the world, and also children without parents."

Did Mother Agnes choose Dickens by design? If so, it was a wise choice. As I read the story of poor Oliver, a workhouse brat, with his endless goodness and monotonous virtues, who remained undefeated though enduring every possible injury, I not only learned English, but discovered England. I also learned a lot about the world and about growing up. Oliver was most definitely English. I was French. We were children of different times and contrasting backgrounds but I could see that we were both pathetic because we were so touching in our naive optimism. We expected others to be kind to us.

Reading Dickens was not easy. Mother Agnes had to explain many unknown and obsolete words. It took me at least two months to achieve any facility in reading English and longer, of course, to be able to write it. Confusion arose when words were the same in both languages but were spelled differently—Ireland, Irlande; address, adresse; sym-

The Ursuline convent, me on the far right, with girls whose names I do not remember. It is difficult for an "alien" to fit in with a group. My only friend was Mother Agnes.

Marguerite and me, in a photo taken in Waterford for our parents, Christmas 1940.

pathy, sympathie. I rapidly became an expert at using my dictionary and loved it as a friend.

Some days the books would be set aside and I would spend my time with the friendly old nun talking about the origin, meaning and spelling of words. These were happy hours, far away from reality and the cruel world, even if it did rain every day.

AT LAST IT WAS DECEMBER and Christmas grew near. News of the war seldom penetrated the thick convent walls and there was no word from home. I wrote often from Waterford and Mr. Horgan and Wally tried as well. For several months at least our parents must not have known where we were.

At long last a letter arrived, bearing the exciting news. Our parents were coming to Ireland for the Christmas holidays. Afterwards, I thought, they would surely take us home. We said goodbye to the students and the nuns as we left for the Christmas holidays, believing we would not be back. As a farewell present, darling Mother Agnes gave me a lovely leather bound "autograph book" and proudly I asked all my friends to sign it. Some of them even took the trouble to add drawings, a verse or an amusing saying. It gave me great happiness.

Wally came to the convent in a hired taxi to pick us up. We drove out to the best hotel of a seaside resort called Tramore to await the arrival of Papa and Maman. Late one evening they appeared, unannounced, and there was a happy reunion. I was so pleased to see my parents again that I could not take my eyes off them. Anxiety was etched across their faces, they did not smile as readily as before and they looked older. But to me, and to Marguerite, they were the most beautiful sight in all the world.

Ireland was a new experience for my parents, totally different, and they were not as at home as they were in England where they had many friends. One afternoon, to our delight, our parents told us that Lady Susan Dawnay, who lived near Waterford, had invited us all for tea. Her son was an officer in the British Army stationed in France at Le Mans, and had visited them at Le Mesnil on several occasions. He had asked them to call on his mother to reassure her of his well-being. Lady Susan Dawnay was happy to see them and receive first hand news of her son.

For the greater part of our visit in the large, friendly, rather untidy drawing-room of Whitfield Court I kept close to my father, drawing a sense of security from his physical nearness. We also played in a great staircase hall with the Dawnay grandchildren and their Beresford, Miller and Girouard cousins. They had a spaniel that could be bribed with a biscuit to walk on his hind legs. This failed to hold my interest for long, and I slipped back behind the sofa on which my mother sat talking to Lady Waterford. Settling behind the chair where my father was talking to Lady Susan Dawnay, I heard him saying in a low solemn voice, "I'm not at all convinced that the Maginot Line is as impregnable as our politicians claim. I don't trust them. This strange war won't last indefinitely; we will soon have a real war and I'm afraid it will be a hard one. . . . No, my wife and I have considered the situation carefully and have decided that it would be in the interest of our daughters' safety for the next few months for them to remain . . ." The voice drifted even lower and I lost the end of the sentence. I had heard enough, and went back to find the other children.

Later my father joined us. "Ah, here you are. Come and sit beside your Papa and tell him with what nonsense Irish nuns have been filling your head!" His manner was disarming, and for a moment banished from my mind all thoughts of what I had just heard.

The day after Christmas our parents told us that we would not be going home with them. We were to go back to school. Arrangements had been made by telephone for us to stay in the Irish convent until June. My parents didn't visit the school because the convent was closed for the

Christmas holidays and Reverend Mother did not wish to be disturbed.

I had managed to push my father's words to Lady Dawnay at Whitfield Court out of mind, but now they flooded back. So this was what had been decided. This was in our best interest, I thought bitterly. I thought of the miserable morning that war had been declared—how totally alone I had felt—and now I was terrified that it would happen again. We were being abandoned for a second time. "It isn't really a very long time. Don't cry. The war will soon be over," said our ever optimistic mother. Marguerite believed her, but for the first time in my life, I did not. I was frightened and miserably unhappy. "It's six months until June," I protested. "Please don't abandon us—don't leave us—I'm only a little girl—I'm only eleven, and Marguerite is the baby of the convent." Nothing I said could make my parents alter their decision.

"We will write to you and see you perhaps at Easter," my mother said in her firm, grown-up way. "It would be such a pity not to finish your school year and you will be safer in Ireland. You will be home for the summer!"

As much as I wanted to, I didn't believe her. Experience had taught me that parents can make mistakes and that, when it suited them, they did not always tell their children the truth. My mother and father disliked "scenes," and I remember very clearly their departure from Tramore. One morning they did not appear in the hotel dining room for breakfast, and when I asked the little waitress if she had seen them, she smiled and cheerfully answered yes—they had left a couple of hours ago, by taxi, with all their luggage. So there was no scene, no crying, no tearful faces. Only Marguerite and I, unable to swallow, staring at each other in silence. Our parents had left without saying goodbye.

Four years would pass without seeing them again or hearing their voices. Even letters would be extremely rare. After the fall of France in June 1940 we had absolutely no news of them for two and a half years. In 1943 an occasional battered letter would arrive via the Red Cross censored by the French, the Germans, sometimes the Swiss or the Portuguese, the English and the Irish. These letters were always very brief, giving us little news, but we took great comfort in them because they told us that at least on the date they were written, several months before, our parents were still alive and we were not really orphans yet.

Sunnyside, the bungalow we lived in for nearly four years.

CHAPTER THREE

Sunnyside

BACK TO THE URSULINE CONVENT went two sad little French girls. Marguerite, always a fragile child and much the youngest of the school, was often in the infirmary. There, by a small fire, she would play with her dolls while a very old nun sat by the window sewing.

I was miserably homesick, apart from the hours when I was either studying with Mother Agnes or running myself breathless on the hockey field. Most girls were kind to me but some of them called me Froggy, my unusual accent being the cause of laughter and some unpleasant teasing.

"Why are you in Ireland, Frog?"

"We have already had the English on our backs. We don't like the French much, you know."

"Reverend Mother says that the French are both dirty and immoral."

In tears, I would run to the safe haven of Mother Agnes's office. "Immoral? Immoral? Please tell me, Mother Agnes, what does that word mean?"

Sometimes Mother Agnes did not know what to say to console me.

The Ursuline convent did however have many good points. The teaching was excellent. Hot water was plentiful, so we all bathed three times a week. The food was very different from the food at Jalesnes but it was just as good and plentiful. We did a lot of "sport" and I particularly loved playing hockey. The dormitory accommodation in the Irish and French schools differed considerably. In France there were two long rows of ten narrow beds for the girls and, at one end of the long room, a white-curtained cubicle for a nun or teacher. In the Irish school, each girl had her own private cubicle and girls of different ages shared the same large space.

One of the older girls, a tall blue-eyed blond with heavy breasts, bore a physical resemblance to my mother. She was always kind to me, often giving me sweets and trying to be with me as much as possible. This was not easy because we had completely different schedules. One day, however, coming back from the infirmary where I had been to see my sister, I met her walking down the corridor.

"Listen," she said, "there is only one place where we can meet and have a really long chat. I want [am longing] to hear all about France and your life there and you could tell me about your father and mother."

"Yes! Where and when?" I asked eagerly. "In the dormitory," whispered the older girl. "It is strictly forbidden, but never mind. Late tonight, come to my cubicle and in my bed, under the warm covers, we'll be able to talk for hours. Don't make any noise. Listen carefully first to make sure everyone is asleep."

This was much too tempting an offer for a homesick and lonely girl to refuse. It really was at last, or so it seemed, the extended hand of friendship.

"Yes," I said happily, "I'll come to your bed tonight. Thank you very much for asking me."

Though the afternoon and evening seemed particularly long, at last it was bedtime. I didn't move until the convent clock struck eleven, as I didn't want my new friend to get into trouble on my account. Noiselessly, on bare feet, I tiptoed down the corridor of cubicles to the one I knew belonged to the tall fair girl. Nobody heard me. Quickly I climbed into the warm bed. She put her arms around me and for a while we talked in low voices to each other.

Then she whispered into my ear: "Close your eyes now and don't move. We will pretend I am your mummy. I am going to kiss you."

I closed my eyes and the older girl began to kiss me in a way my mother never did. I began to tremble. "No," I said, and started to climb out of the bed.

She held my arm firmly. "Don't go, I want you to caress my breasts. It can be very nice, you know." By now I was trembling from head to toe and my teeth were chattering.

"I'm going back to my bed," I said.

In a hushed but furious voice she whispered. "Go away then, if you want to. I don't really care because you are just a dirty French frog anyway."

I was so innocent that I did not understand why, in the days that followed, she did all she could to make me miserable.

The following week I had a terrible pain in my tummy. I was nervy, feverish, and had a bad headache. After the English class I told the teacher that I wasn't feeling well and she sent me to the infirmary. There the nurse put me to bed with a hot water bottle. She gave me a pill to swallow and told me that I was going to have my period, better known to my friends as "the curse." It appeared the next morning. I was both disgusted and upset. I felt that *le ciel était tombé sur ma tête*—the sky had fallen on my head—but then luckily for me and perhaps because of the ongoing stress, my "curse" totally disappeared for several years.

But the worst was still to come. At tea time on a sunny day in June, the girls and the nuns were quieter than usual. That evening, staring at me just across the tea table, my new enemy bent forward and in a clear voice so that everyone at the table could hear said, "We all know, and it has once again been proved, that the French are a race of cowards. There is a great battle being fought and they are running like rabbits in front of the victorious Germans."

She had barely finished her sentence when I was on my feet slapping her astonished face with all my strength. Then, breathless with rage, I ran to the security of Mother Agnes's office where I collapsed in tears. She was very kind when she heard the story of "the French cowards." She said that, had she not been a nun, she would have done the same thing under the circumstances.

As Mother Agnes was also very brave, she promised that she would go and see Reverend Mother Aloysius, who terrified nuns and girls alike, and tell her my story to ensure that I would not be too severely punished or expelled.

My fury could not banish from my mind, however, that horrid girl's words about a battle raging and the French being on the run. Fear for my parents and family, which I had barely managed to contain, came boiling to the surface. With the calamitous news on the 14th of June that German troops were marching past the Arc de Triomphe and parading down the Champs Elysées, feelings of desolation overwhelmed me.

Even my end-of-year report, which was described by the nuns as "astonishingly good," failed to bring any spark of joy or even to interest me. The nuns saw me as a serious twelve-year-old child. They did not know that I would always be haunted by the memory of a cold deserted September beach; that I was terrified of what would happen next. Two days before the school was due to close for the long summer holiday Wally arrived at the convent for an interview with the reverend mother, a thin little woman with a cruel mouth. Wally explained that she was now our "guardian for the duration of the war." She had hardly any money, only our now useless passports and our equally useless return tickets to France.

"Would you be kind enough," she asked, "to keep the girls for a few days longer until I find some money and an inexpensive place to spend the summer?"

"No," said Reverend Mother, "definitely not. You must understand, Miss Walsh, that next week we are organizing our yearly retreat for former students, and there is no earthly reason why this convent should go to the expense of keeping two French refugees a day longer than their parents have paid for."

Wally then asked to see us. It was in the small, dreary, well-polished convent parlor that we heard from this hysterical middle-aged woman that once again we were penniless, that we might never see our home or our parents again, and that we were now alien refugees. We would have to leave the convent on the same day as the other girls, the difference being that unlike them, we had nowhere to go. We were in a sorry plight. We had no country, no family, no friends, no money. Our very existence depended on human charity, and for the first time in my life I was learning that it could not be taken for granted. Yet a solution was close at hand.

Both Lady Susan Dawnay and Lady Waterford provided immediate aid by lending Wally some money. They also offered us refuge in their large comfortable houses, along with their protection and the company of their children, grandchildren, dogs and ponies. After all, we were children, and possibly the only ones in such a predicament in the entire Republic of Ireland that summer.

This was the obvious and perfect solution. Our parents were not without friends, and by extension nor were we. But, alas, no. It would have been too easy, too normal, too wonderfully simple to have accepted their hospitality for our holidays or even longer. Wally's response was an emphatic, resounding "No." It was entirely beyond my comprehension, and left me shaken and bewildered.

To agree to this generous and appropriate offer was apparently unthinkable to Wally. Lady Susan Dawnay and Lady Waterford were Protestants. Wally's upbringing had been based on the core teaching and belief that, in Ireland, Catholics and Protestants must never mix. This was so completely foreign to me, with my family's casual approach to religious matters, that I had not even the language to discuss it with Wally had she been willing to listen, which she was not. Her opinions on this subject were as fixed as her faith was perfect. Years later I was to discover with bittersweet irony that my mother's own family on her father's side were French Protestants. And so was my godmother.

"What exactly is a Protestant?" I asked her. "Why cannot we stay with them for the summer? If you really don't like them, why do you accept their money? To me it doesn't make sense."

To these questions, Wally gave this answer: "Protestants are the enemies of good Catholics. They always have been and always will be. We hate them, and the sooner you know it the better."

"Oh God," I sighed under my breath, beginning to wonder to which church He belonged. Sad Ireland, Holy Ireland. It was a lot of nonsense I could not understand. Such intolerance left me in flabbergasted silence.

*A*FTER BREAKFAST ON THE LAST DAY of the summer term, school discipline degenerated rapidly. The imminent arrival of parents vanquished all other thoughts. The effect was hypnotic. Girls assembled in the main hall, glassy-eyed, sleepwalking, looking with unseeing eyes straight at friends with whom they had been in close company for months. All thoughts were of home, as though this had been merely a long interruption in real life. Uniformed figures of various sizes and shapes entered the hall burdened by suitcases which were then placed on the floor at odd angles, contributing to the general disorder. I watched as one girl limped in dragging an overflowing suitcase displaying bits and ends of various items of clothing. When she tripped over a protruding shaft of a hockey stick, she picked herself up and continued on her way as if nothing unusual had happened.

At first there were no nuns in evidence, but they gradually appeared and helped as guides, threading a path through the general disarray, ushering parents to where their eager daughters were waiting. Never will I forget that morning. Of all our fellows, we were pointedly unexpectant. We were painfully not waiting for parents whom we knew would not come, knowing that we had no place to go. Marguerite and I stood close together in a corner of the hall, a tiny, overlooked and desolate island in that flood of joyful family groups.

Marguerite, pale and in a daze, not really understanding, hugged her favorite doll as we stood unnoticed beside the two little suitcases that held our few schoolgirl treasures, my autograph book, my diary and the few pieces of clothing that seemed to grow a little shorter and tighter with every passing day. I looked around, at the hall's cold, gray, unfriendly bare walls; at the high door with a large black crucifix hanging above it. I thought that the face of Christ wore a look of despair rather than one of compassion and that cries of "long live the holidays" were certainly not for us.

"I won't regret this blinking place," I said to myself, with a shiver. At that moment, kind Mother Agnes, whom I would greatly miss, arrived to say goodbye. Her eyes filled with tears as she kissed us and asked us to write to her. Then I asked her if we should say goodbye to Reverend Mother Superior. "I will ask," she said. She came back right away. The answer was "No, she is much too busy with the other girls' parents and organizing the retreat."

That is how at the ages of nine and twelve, Marguerite and I found ourselves once again abandoned, this time on an Irish street in the city of Waterford.

When Wally eventually arrived, we silently obeyed her orders, dragging our suitcases behind us and feeling miserable. At the Waterford station we climbed into the dingy second-class compartment of a dusty train.

"Where are you taking us? Where are we going?" I asked, in a worried voice.

"You'll see. I managed to borrow a little money for the summer," she answered. She did not say from whom—but opened her bag and smiled a strange smile at both of us as she lit one of her endless cigarettes.

*W*HAT I DID NOT THEN FULLY UNDERSTAND was that now both England and Ireland were isolated from the European continent and that we would no longer receive any news, money or letters from our parents, who were now trapped in Occupied France.

Trains in Ireland, in 1940, were very slow, stopping seemingly at random at villages or farmhouses right out in the middle of the countryside. After several hours, we arrived at the little town of Dungarvan. It was towards the end of market day and cattle remained on streets that were littered with straw and slippery with dung. Drunken men were standing—or more precisely leaning—against the walls of the local pubs. They had thick tweed caps sitting on their heads and it was difficult to tell whether their red faces, shining with warmth, were the result of the quantities of Guinness they had drunk or from the warm sunshine. I suspected the stout was the stronger of the two.

Children were playing in the street—thin, red-headed with lots of freckles. None wore shoes. Their feet were large, wide and dirty. This surprised me as I had never seen children without shoes, even in Brittany where they sometimes wore clogs. Their clothes were neither washed nor mended—except perhaps with large pins. There were many very young girls carrying infants in their arms and wearing, as did their mothers, black shawls over their heads and shoulders. We stared at them and they stared back.

Suddenly there was a commotion in the direction of a little bakery. A nanny goat, seeing an open door, had entered the shop and was now being dragged by the tail into the street by a small boy who was pulling with all his might. Both the boy and goat were making a tremendous noise. The onlookers were either laughing or protesting loudly and giving advice.

At last Wally found the car she had hired. It was owned by a fat man who never stopped talking in a heavy Irish brogue which I could barely understand. He drove exuberantly out of the town and in a perilously carefree fashion along a winding and narrow road out to the tiny seaside resort of Clonea Strand. We sat silently in the back seat, steeping in its strange and nasty smell. I quietly opened the window.

In Clonea, distinguished by its whitewashed walls, stood a hotel owned by a Mrs. Monahan, a middle-aged widow. The Ocean View, as it was called, faced the Atlantic across a long sandy beach that swept up to a barricade of shingles against which, at high tide, the waves would break. Behind the shingles, bordered first by a field and then a high stone wall, were half a dozen small wooden bungalows, painted in various cheerful shades of yellow, pink and green. There were no trees—only a few hollyhocks and marigolds growing wild.

These bungalows, in effect only summer beach huts, were built in a row with their backs to the stone wall and ocean. They overlooked a large bog on the other side of which was a winding road that led either to Dungarvan or to Waterford. In the distance to the north rose the beautiful heather-covered Comeragh and Monavullagh mountains which were blazed pink and mauve in the setting sun. Often after rain they were crowned by rainbows.

Wally had rented a small room in the hotel with three narrow beds and a window overlooking the backyard. My sister and I spent most days on the cold and windy beach, still speaking French from time to time to each other. The Irish children did not ask us to play. Possibly the unfamiliar sound of French kept them at a distance, but there also must have been something else. We were sad, we were worried, we really did not want to play, and they sensed it. So we spent most of our time sitting on a jetty of rocks gazing out to sea.

One day, when at last the sun appeared, two young Irish girls came and sat beside us.

"My name is Patsy," said the eldest girl, "and this is my sister Molly. We'll be starting to learn French next year. Our mother told us to come and talk to you so that you could teach us some words."

"Of course," I answered. "We can teach you lots of words. Where shall we start?"

"Simple phrases—the ones you use most. How do you say 'please' in French?"

"S'il vous plait."

"How do you do?"

"Bonjour."

"Goodbye?"

"Au revoir."

"Thank you?"

"Mer . . . merde!" I said suddenly feeling terribly homesick.

"Merde," repeated Molly absolutely perfectly. "How do you say 'thank you very much'?"

"Easy," answered Marguerite, joining in the game. "You say 'Merde beaucoup.' "

We both were having difficulty suppressing our giggles as our new Irish friends left us saying, "See you tomorrow and merde beaucoup, merde beaucoup."

When they had left, Marguerite and I rolled down the shingle onto the white sand of the beach, laughing as we had not laughed for a long time.

For several minutes I lay on the warm beach slowly sifting the silky sand over my arms, onto my legs and between my brown fingers until I found a seashell. I put it to my ear and listened to its whispering of other shores—Brittany shores. Feeling strangely happy and being careful not to move I listened to my heart and my heart told me that the sun and the sand were universal and belonged to every living thing.

It was while staying in the Clonea Ocean View Hotel that we first heard the voice of Winston Churchill. We listened then, as we would listen for the next four years, in awed silence. Mr. Churchill said that in the end Great Britain and her allies would win the war, that good would overcome evil and that to lose a battle did not mean that the war was lost. He promised victory, but before that day there would be "blood, toil, tears and sweat."

His voice brought hope. He spoke to me in words I understood, rather than in the depressing and opaque patter of Wally. I believed him and was convinced. I would see my country and my parents again. From that moment, my admiration for the British people, who were so brave and determined to fight, was boundless. I did not know much about blood, toil or sweat, but of tears I knew a great deal. I had shed many and knew many more could flow. And so I made a secret vow. My private battle would be the battle of tears and I promised Mr. Churchill that I would not cry again until the end of the war. I thought it would be unfair if grown-up people, who had so much to do, also had weeping children on their hands. If Mr. Churchill and his friends could manage the blood, sweat and toil, then I could manage the tears.

I did not speak to the grown-ups in the hotel who were also listening raptly to the wireless. They looked very glum and some said that they would cut short their holidays. They seemed pleased that Ireland was "neutral" and that they would be safe. I did not clearly understand what "neutral" meant. What I knew was that Ireland was an island and that I could not run home to France. "It's hard," I thought, "to be only twelve years old and a girl."

On the 8th of August, wave upon successive wave of German planes appeared in the skies over Britain unleashing millions of tons of explosives on the main seaports and cities of England, Scotland, Wales and Northern Ireland. Thousands of civilians were killed, thousands more were wounded. The terrifying sounds of the Battle of Britain came out of the radio—we could hear the air raid warnings, the exploding bombs, the ambulances and then the "all clear."

The Royal Air Force counterattacked, the pilots and their crews showing such extraordinary bravery and endurance that they would enter forever into both history and legend. In the course of ten days, seven hundred German planes were destroyed. Huddled by the radio, we listened and held our breath. The final outcome of the war now

seemed undecided and on August 20th, the voice of Mr.
Churchill resounded once again from the radio in the dining room of our hotel. Like many other people I will never
forget either his voice or his words: "Never in the field of
human conflict was so much owed by so many to so few."

BY THE END OF AUGUST 1940, money was getting scarce
again and Wally didn't know what to do. She told me
she didn't have enough money to cover the hotel bill and I
wondered if we would be sent to prison to work off our
food. I suggested that she write to Lord Derby who she
knew was a friend of our parents. She was too proud to ask
Lady Waterford for his address, or perhaps at this point she
didn't want to disturb her. I told Wally just to write on the
envelope "Lord Derby, England." For days she fretted
nervously, moaning that the letter would never reach its
destination and that we had no money to pay Mrs. Monahan; that I was a foolish child to think that anything could
be sent that way. But I believed in the English and in
Mr. Churchill. They would find a way.

Lord Derby was both famous and well loved, and the
English post office, even during the height of the blitz, very
efficient. Within two weeks we received an answer, and
with the letter came a check for £100, a fortune in those
days. It was more money than I had ever seen.

Also, in his letter, Lord Derby invited Wally and us to
come to Knowsley, his country estate, and live with him
and his wife until the end of the war. Once again Wally refused, on the pretext that since Ireland was a neutral country, we were safer here. It might have been better if the good
earl had simply sent sea and rail tickets instead of cash. She
made me write a "thank you" letter, carefully correcting my
spelling to make sure that Lord Derby would know she was
a first-class governess, and that we were safe in her capable
hands. She remained in command, and made certain that
she did not lose her wartime job.

The day after the check arrived, Wally rented one of the bungalows on Clonea Strand at £30 for the year. The bungalow was very small but optimistically called "Sunnyside." It was built of wood and the outside was painted yellow while the interior walls were simply varnished. It was sparsely furnished with simple wooden pieces and short transparent cotton curtains hanging in the windows. It had neither electricity nor running water. There was no bathroom. The lavatory was outside, down three steps from the kitchen door. There were two bedrooms. Wally decided to share the larger one with Marguerite and I would have, to my great relief, the smaller one to myself. In the center of the bungalow was a small living room with a fireplace, a cupboard, a square table covered with an oilcloth, and four chairs. The kitchen contained a stove but no sink, a table and four more chairs. There was also a back room for the empty suitcases and a glass porch in front of the living room which looked out over the bog toward the mountains. From inside it was impossible to see the sea, but it could always be heard, growling, especially at high tide. Rainwater, which was nothing if not plentiful, was collected from the roof into a large wooden barrel and was used for everything except drinking. There was a hole in the nearby sandy field to bury the rubbish. Seeing Sunnyside for the first time I thought it desperately bleak. I knew Wally herself to be such a cold woman that it would be a miracle if we did not catch pneumonia just from living under the same small roof alone with her.

Wally had not talked to us or consulted anyone when she decided to rent this bungalow and use Lord Derby's money to pay a year's rent in advance. As soon as we were settled, however, she wrote to Lady Waterford telling her what she had done and asking her to come to tea.

She baked a sponge cake and made some trifle. Lady Waterford came, looked over the house and then sat down for tea. After two cups, no food and a long silence, she said to Wally, who had bravely refrained from lighting a cigarette, "Have you realized that Clonea Strand is five Irish

The gate at Sunnyside, and our outdoor lavatory, which consisted of a hole in a wooden plank and rainwater in a bucket.

miles from Dungarvan? Where will the children go to school?"

"They will not go to school," answered Wally in a firm voice. "I am now not only their governess but also their guardian. I have a letter from their mother saying so. I will teach them myself."

I looked at her with horror. "Damn it," I murmured under my breath as I realized the implication. We were prisoners, and would stay prisoners of Wally for the duration of the war. There was to be no escape. I could not bring myself to believe that Maman had written such a letter, and it was the first I had heard of it. Lady Waterford looked very worried but raised no objection. She was herself a young widow, with two small boys and a large property to manage. She had only met my parents once, and had no legal footing to challenge the arrangement, although Sunnyside clearly horrified her. She ate nothing and stayed not fifteen minutes. That night was the first night that I had a great deal of trouble keeping my secret promise to Mr. Churchill.

The arrival a few days later of three bicycles kindly lent to us by Lady Waterford was a happy event. Soon after, Lady Susan Dawnay sent us a wireless so that we could follow the war news. It worked on a heavy battery and we only listened to it in the evening, first to "Children's Hour" and then the news.

To MARGUERITE'S ASTONISHMENT and my despair, one by one the owners of the other bungalows closed them around the middle of September, most of them returning to the nearby town of Clonmel. "We'll be coming back next July," they said, cheerfully, as we watched them depart in the pouring rain.

At the end of the Strand the only remaining cottage was occupied by Johnny and Johanna Maloney, an elderly Irish couple with no children who had lived for many years in their one room with a peat fire in the only chimney.

They spoke mostly Irish to each other. The Ocean View Hotel also closed its doors. Kind Mrs. Monahan said she would open the dining room on Sundays. Otherwise there was not a single human being in the whole of Clonea Strand.

On the black winter nights of 1940–41, German bombers started flying regularly over southern Ireland on their way north toward Belfast. The bombers would arrive from the sea, following a skypath over Clonea Strand, the bog and the mountains that led them to the industrial towns and ports of Northern Ireland. As they flew towards their targets, the heavily loaded planes advanced slowly, their engines humming in a low, forbidding key. On their homeward journey, their deadly mission accomplished, they flew faster, much faster, the notes of the engines high-pitched in a hysterical scream.

As soon as the bombers had passed above Clonea Strand and were over the ocean, those that still carried bombs dropped them into the sea, where they exploded. The first night this happened, Wally, my sister and I were terrified. We stood barefoot in our nighties, huddled together in the living room. When silence returned, after making certain that the curtains overlapped each window, Wally lit a candle.

"How close do you think those bombs fell?" asked Marguerite, her face pale green and trembling with fear.

"About a couple of miles away, I think," answered Wally. "The windows aren't broken."

"I hate the Germans," I murmured, trying to sound brave but much more frightened than I cared to admit.

Wally then lit the primus—the little camping stove that ran cheaply on paraffin—and we drank hot tea before returning to our beds, still shaking from this new and unexpected ordeal.

Wally bicycled into Dungarvan the next day to ask for an explanation as to why the Germans had dropped bombs into the sea.

"It is quite simple," she was told. "Those were the

bombs that they didn't have time to drop on Belfast before being attacked by RAF fighters. By dropping them into the ocean, the German planes become much lighter and faster, helping their chances of escape from the pursuing British Hurricanes and Spitfires. There is really nothing to be frightened about."

I took little comfort from this but hoped Marguerite was convinced. I couldn't help thinking that there was always the possibility of a German navigator miscalculating and that, if the bombs fell only a few seconds too soon, we would be killed. There wasn't even a cellar at Sunnyside to take refuge in. But it was wise not to dwell on such thoughts, and certainly unkind to share them. We never did become accustomed to the Germans flying overhead. After the first bombing, Wally bought black cotton luster to make our flowered curtains opaque and this was the occasion of my first sewing lesson. After a time, I began trying to count the number of planes going up, and those—sometimes fewer— coming back, and the number of explosions occurring just off the coast. At least those bombs, I thought, even if they frightened us, had not carried death to Belfast.

THE TRAVELING GROCER, who had made a weekly visit to Clonea Strand during the summer months, stopped coming. It became necessary to bicycle the five Irish miles into Dungarvan for food. We set off riding into a strong wind on a narrow road and over a crooked bridge. The journey took hours, and the road back seemed twice as long. To add to our misery it started to drizzle and it was raining heavily when at last we arrived at Sunnyside with our purchases. Marguerite was in a state of collapse and Wally was torn between fatigue and bad temper. Not wishing a weekly repetition of this experience, she reconsidered the group expedition.

"Sylvia," she said, "you are the strongest, so from now on you will do the shopping in Dungarvan. You will go there once a week, and I will also go from time to time. I shall write out a list of things to buy and you will have to be very careful not to lose any money. You will give me back the change and I will keep the accounts." Keeping meticulous track of the "accounts" was very important to Wally, though the sums were tiny, convinced as she was that she would have to show them to our parents after the war.

The following week I left Clonea Strand early in the morning to do our shopping. I had Wally's list and one Irish pound note carefully folded in my purse. I was to purchase cigarettes, bread, butter, bacon, tea and meat for an Irish stew. A pair of shoes which were being repaired was also to be collected. To start with the shoes and finish at the butcher's shop was the obvious course. It was a fine sunny autumn day and my shopping progressed faster than I had expected. My bicycle was in good condition and the half-moon shaped basket on the handlebars soon filled with my purchases. There was only the meat to buy and then I could head back.

I had never before been inside a butcher's shop so I stopped first on the other side of the street, sitting on my black bicycle peddling backwards for a few minutes. I watched a woman wearing a shawl go in the door and come out with a small parcel. Simple enough. In a happy frame of mind I entered Mr. Flynn's shop and politely asked him for a pound of mutton for the weekly stew. As I stood at the counter, I became aware of a peculiar odor. It was a bizarre smell and it was turning my stomach. Mr. Flynn had blood on his hands and there were bloodstains on his apron and on the sawdust that covered the floor.

I began to feel distinctly unwell. "Are you one of the French girls living out in Clonea Strand?" asked Mrs. Flynn, who was sitting on a high chair behind a cash machine. I looked up toward her to answer, but at that moment I saw, hanging just above her left shoulder, a naked lamb whose tongue was hanging out of his mouth. Fresh blood was all over him still and his eyes were curiously alive. I stared at the lamb in horror, unable to break away from the sad brown eyes. The shop began to spin. Mr. and Mrs. Flynn and the dead animal disappeared into a haze—I slid limply to the ground in a dead faint, like a brown leaf on winter snow.

When I opened my eyes, I found myself on a large double bed in a strange room. Against the light from the window, I could see the shape of a woman bending over me.

"Feeling better now, are you?" said the woman.

"Oui, merci, je me sens un peu mieux. Pouvez-vous me donner un verre d'eau, s'il vous plait?" I asked. There was no answer. I had asked for a glass of water in my native tongue.

"Come on now, dearie," said the woman, in a soft Irish brogue. "You'll be all right, please be to God. Sit up, dearie. I'll make ye a nice hot cup o'tea, very strong with lots of sugar."

Gently coaxing me, still half dazed, off the bed, she guided me with maternal kindness by the arm toward the kitchen. "Sit on that chair. You'll be fine in a minute. I'll give you a slice o'cake and here's the strong cup o'tea. I know what children like—I've had nine of them meself, God bless them, you know."

Color was coming back to my face and I was beginning to feel better.

"How old are you?" asked Mrs. Flynn, anxiously. I saw that she was not very tall but very plump. Her hair was going gray and she had a kind face, but it was the tenderness in her voice that I liked. "Twelve," I answered.

"How come you fainted, little one? Didn't that governess of yours give you a proper breakfast?"

"Oh yes, I had breakfast all right, I had my porridge. I'm terribly sorry to have fainted, Mrs. Flynn. But you see, I've never been in a butcher's shop before. The naked sheep gave me a shock. I thought that he was still alive."

Mrs. Flynn threw back her head and roared with laughter. "Michael," she shouted to her husband, "you'll never believe it. The child fainted because she had never been in a butcher's shop before—that's the funniest thing

I've heard in many a day. Glory be to God, we cannot have her fainting on us every week. Listen to me, little one. Don't come into the shop again. Ring your bicycle bell by the door and Mr. Flynn will give you what you need out of the window."

"Oh, thank you," I said, feeling ashamed of myself for having fainted. "Please, Mrs. Flynn, please don't tell my governess I fainted. I know that she would not like it."

Mrs. Flynn promised not to tell her. Mr. Flynn handed me the parcel of mutton carefully wrapped in newspaper and then put six pennies in my hand "to buy sweets." I handed the pennies back. "No, I'm terribly sorry, but Miss Walsh won't let us accept charity."

"Charity," laughed Mr. Flynn handing the coins back again. "Don't be silly, go and buy yourself some sweets and just don't tell Miss Walsh a thing."

He winked at me in such a friendly, fatherly way that there was nothing I could do but accept the money and say thank you. I went straight back to the grocery shop and bought myself two pence worth of sweets and saved the rest.

"I must be very careful with money," I said to myself. This I had found out quite a while ago.

Mrs. Flynn didn't tell Wally that I had fainted but she did tell a friend, who in turn told someone else, who then told Wally. As I had rightly guessed, Wally was furious.

"How dare you faint. You have made yourself ridiculous," she shouted. "I'll teach you not to faint and be such a coward. From now on until the end of the war, you will always buy all the meat that comes into this house. Fainting indeed! Don't you ever do it again."

I didn't answer. I had no cause for worry because of kind Mr. Flynn's arrangement with the bicycle bell. Also, it was no use arguing with a furious Wally. She seemed more menacing and more stupid than ever. Anyway, as the months went by, there would be less and less meat as rationing became the norm. It started with petrol for lighting and for cars. Then, tea and sugar. Butter, meat, white flour and cigarettes would all become scarcer as the bread became blacker. The fact that we had little money and no family did not help.

Once installed in the little yellow cottage at Clonea Strand, Wally decided for reasons of economy to cut our hair herself. One morning she sat Marguerite on the kitchen table with a towel around her neck. "Now don't move" she said, waving an old pair of scissors, and she began cutting into my sister's thick auburn curls. I watched her attentively. It was quite evident that Wally did not have a natural talent for hairdressing. As she hacked at my sister's head, Marguerite's eyes getting larger by the minute, I made a decision about my own hair. In a firm tone of voice I stated, "I want to let my hair grow. I shall have pigtails. They are both practical and neat."

As Wally had found cutting my sister's hair tiresome, she miraculously agreed. Thus two silky blond pigtails grew and reached the middle of my back in the course of the following years while poor Marguerite, who had her hairdo "refreshed" regularly, never had even length hair on each side of her face. This gave her a strange lopsided look, her head appearing to lean sometimes to the left and sometimes to the right, that she was to sport for the rest of our years in Ireland.

AT THE END OF SEPTEMBER, Wally started giving us lessons. When she had arrived in France in 1938, it was to look after and teach a seven-year-old child. More advanced capacities were now required. I had reached the age of bubbling curiosity about everything and it was within minutes after beginning her first lesson that Wally realized she was facing unforeseen difficulties. Pride and obstinacy fortified her against any nagging doubts which might have assailed her mind.

"I will give you each a long dictation. Any mistakes in

spelling will be punished and you will have to copy the word, correctly spelled, a hundred times because spelling is very important. Afterwards we will do some arithmetic."

"Grammar," I said, "is surely more important than spelling. That is what Mademoiselle Marthe always said, I remember very well."

Wally's answer was short and to the point, "Shut up." The question of grammar was left at that.

Wally sat between us at the square table in the living-room. Opening my Waterford convent English book, she read a dictation in her firm voice. I was told to check it over while she read a shorter and easier one to Marguerite. Then, with the help of the book, which I noticed she glanced at from time to time, she carefully corrected both dictations, giving us each the misspelled words to write out a hundred times. While we did, Wally prepared the arithmetic lesson. It consisted of two long additions, two subtractions, and a multiplication for me, and two simple additions for Marguerite. I studied the sums carefully. They were very easy. I only had to chew on the end of my pencil a couple of times.

When I had finished, I handed them to Wally saying, "They were quite simple. I don't think that I've made a mistake. Now give me some divisions and fractions. I started algebra and geometry in school; can we try some of those, please?" A change came over Wally's face, like the sudden change on the surface of the sea when the sun disappeared behind a cloud, as it often did in Clonea Strand. She looked very cross.

"If these sums are too easy for you, I will give you more difficult ones, but nothing else. Algebra and geometry are quite useless."

As the lessons progressed, it became evident that Wally had forgotten how to do division and had never been taught fractions, algebra or geometry. The multiplication tables became Wally's predominant theme. We recited them continuously, in singsong voices, with Wally keeping a close eye on the book watching for mistakes.

One day Wally decided to add French dictation to the

mind-numbing routine. Sitting at the table holding a book that had belonged to Mother Agnes, Wally read and I bent over my copy book and began to write. All went well for the first sentences. Then it gradually became clear to me that something extremely odd was happening. Wally spoke English with a carefully cultivated English accent that I suppose she thought was upper-crust, but in her halting French a strong Irish brogue that obviously came straight from County Waterford reasserted itself in spectacular fashion. This assault on my ears struck me as unbelievably funny. I looked up and saw Wally, rapt in concentration over the text. My giggle started softly. I tried valiantly to suppress it and failed. Soon I could not stop laughing.

Wally was beside herself. This French brat was attempting to humiliate her, she thought, although it was not the case. I was merely laughing at her accent. She stood up, grasped me by the shoulders, gave me a good shake, hit me and then released me with a push that sent me tumbling against the wall at the other side of the room. That was the first and last French lesson in the yellow bungalow.

The inevitable English dictation and simple sums continued each day without variation. I became very bored.

"Why don't we do some grammar? Why don't we study history and geography?" I asked hopefully.

"Grammar is not important; spelling is. History and geography are not important and in any case I don't have money to buy these books, but next time I go to Dungarvan, I will buy a secondhand book of English poetry so that you can be properly educated."

Wally had boundless faith in the educational value of poetry. She kept her promise and three days later bought *The Casket of Gems,* a collection by different poets.

"This evening," she said, "you will learn a poem written by William Wordsworth, 'The Daffodils.' " I was soon reciting the first verse.

> *I wander'd lonely as a cloud*
> *That floats on high o'er vales and hills*

> *When all at once I saw a crowd,*
> *A host, of golden daffodils.*

This was a welcome diversion. It was good exercise for my memory and stimulated my badly starved imagination.

"I want to go back to school, any school. Why can't I go to school in Dungarvan? There is surely a girl's school there. Please."

"Firstly, Dungarvan is five miles away and secondly, there are schools there but as most of the teaching is in Irish, it is of no use to anyone. I don't speak Irish myself. You couldn't follow the classes. They do not want to have you and it would be a waste of time. You are much better off here."

There was no alternative—though I learned long after that it was completely untrue that the classes were taught in Irish. We had to carry on with Wally's dreary lessons, which continued for the next two years. At least I enjoyed the poems and I learned by heart, from cover to cover, *The Casket of Gems*. It never seems to have occurred to Wally to buy another book, though if it had, there was always the problem of money.

Things could have been different. One day we received a friendly letter from the Reverend Mother Superior Aloysius of the Ursuline convent who said she had heard that we were not going to school. Clearly someone had spoken to her—perhaps Mr. Horgan, whose daughter had stayed several years with the nuns. She was prepared to take us both back as boarders until the end of the war for no money, putting off the issue of tuition. I pleaded with Wally to let us go back, the nuns now seeming kind and generous in retrospect, and I loved Mother Agnes. Wally refused, and sent no reply to the reverend mother's letter. When I insisted, she burned it. I had never felt for a moment that Wally loved either of us, or that she was prepared to do what might be best for our education and our future, but now her simple agenda was wholly clear. Her only priority was to preserve her job. She forbade me to write to Mother Agnes.

THE FOLLOWING WEEK I realized that Marguerite was ill. She had no temperature but had stopped playing with her doll. She sat on a chair all day staring out the window at nothing in particular. She seldom spoke. When she refused to eat Wally finally took notice and went into Dungarvan for medical advice. She came back loaded down with bottles of stout. She gave Marguerite a bottle a day for several weeks. The dark stout with its white foam collar made my little sister fall sound asleep after each meal. I also thought that she was often rather drunk, as what she said did not make much sense. But it seemed to cure her because after a while her strength was restored and she started to eat and play again.

When Marguerite had recovered her health, Wally decided that we would go to Mass every Sunday. We had not been since the Ursuline convent, but with the loan of the three bicycles from Lady Dawnay, it was now feasible. Wally had found a church in the middle of the country about two miles inland from Clonea Strand, at a place called Garranbane.

On a warm autumn morning we set off, dressed in our best clothes, now distinctly too short and too tight. The bicycle ride was longer than Wally had thought, not because of the distance but because the road was narrow with many potholes, and wound uphill the entire way toward the heather covered mountains. Weather-beaten old trees mingled with a hedge that at least protected us from the wind. On the way we passed several small farmhouses, but the main road was entirely without traffic. Finally, we rounded a bend and a lovely little church popped unexpectedly into view, nestled in a cemetery crowded with graves and a small forest of Celtic crosses.

People were arriving from different directions, on foot, on bicycles, in donkey carts. There was one small black car belonging to the priest and looking very out of place. Slowly the crowd grew. As I looked at the children I noticed that some of them were wearing shoes. The women had black shawls over their heads and the younger women, as in Dungarvan, were holding babies in their arms. The men in tweed suits were bare headed or had flat tweed caps pulled forward over their eyes. As we arrived they all stared at us, and spoke to each other in low voices. Some pointed and laughed. We were strangers and I felt uncomfortable. The bell rang and we walked into the small church.

Wally took us to a pew quite near the altar. The church filled up until every seat was occupied and the back and sides were filled with standing men. Mass began and the familiar Latin made me relax. It must have been a special feast day because I remember the smoke and the aroma of incense. It did not, however, mask a more pungent smell, far stronger and extremely nasty. It seemed to grow thicker until I could almost feel it in my nose and throat. There was no fresh air, and I began to feel sick. Mass was proceeding ever so slowly. I looked at Wally, who seemed quite undisturbed. I could not see my sister, who was on her other side. Then as the incense was put away the other stronger human body smell grew more intense. "Wally," I said, "I am going to faint." She glared at me flabbergasted. "Don't you dare," she said, grabbing me by my shoulder, and with Marguerite in tow, she got me out just in time.

The fresh air revived me as we rode downhill to Clonea Strand. We never went back to that little church. I did not dare ask Wally what that dreadful smell was. I had guessed, and peddling down the hill, cheerfully thought up a naughty little poem to share with Marguerite, who must have suffered as much as I.

> *Oh now, to be sure isn't it great—*
> *Thanks be to God and his Holy Mother—*
> *that the saintly Irish in their faith,*
> *Do not worship soap and water!*
> *Amen.*

NOVEMBER DAYLIGHT WAS MUCH SHORTER in our remote corner of Ireland than it was in France. One evening Marguerite and I were sitting at the living-room table. Wally had given us each a rag and we were busy polishing with great care the copper of the oil lamp, the long narrow and delicate glass tube and the round belly. In order to have proper light, the lamp had to be perfectly clean. It was fun making the copper shine. Suddenly, through the window, we saw two policemen, known as "guards," walking toward the bungalow. In this deserted locality, their sudden appearance was both unusual and unnerving. Apprehensively, I answered the loud knock on the door.

"We want to see Miss Walsh," said the taller man. "Are you Miss Walsh?" he asked as Wally came out of the kitchen.

"Yes," she answered.

"You know that you are living here with two aliens. We have come to tell you that on the first Monday of every month they will have to report to the police station and sign a special book that has now been opened for the registration of aliens. Also, they must not travel more than ten miles away from this region without letting us know."

"How old are you?" he asked me.

"I am twelve and a half and my sister is nine and a half."

"All right. From now on, you'll have to come and sign our book on the first Monday of every month."

Addressing himself to Wally, he added, "Just send the older girl. They don't both have to come. The police station is on the other side of Dungarvan, about half a mile out."

"If ever you forget to come and sign," he said crossly, turning back to me, "you will all be in trouble. We are on the lookout for foreign spies. Good afternoon."

I stared at them silently, wondering if at the age of twelve I would make a good spy. They walked away along the bog toward their car on the small road by Johnny Maloney's cottage.

Financial anxieties increased with the approach of

Sunnyside, a wooden summer bungalow between the Atlantic Ocean and a bog, with no trees, five miles from Dungarvan.

winter. Money was draining away in spite of our rigid economies. The first week of December I was still wearing a cotton summer dress that was already too short, a hand-knitted sweater and an old pair of sandals.

Wally said that I would have to wear the sandals all winter because they would be too small by next summer. New shoes were out of the question. I could still wear my rubber boots, and in the bungalow we went barefoot. I hoped that my feet wouldn't grow too fast. At least my legs were still suntanned, giving an appearance of warmth, but bicycling into Dungarvan it was difficult to ignore that winter was coming, with the hostile east wind blowing over the flat and desolate bog.

On the first Monday in December, a little shy and very nervous, I walked into the Dungarvan police station for the first time. Two guards were sitting at a wide desk playing cards. I recognized the one I had seen at Clonea Strand. Remembering me, he left the game and collected a large black book from the counter. He opened it at the first page and handed me a pen. I carefully wrote in my childish handwriting my name, age, religion, sex, and address, all the while mumbling angrily to myself about the great stupidity of grown-up people.

"Nice little girls don't swear," scolded the guard.

"I'm not swearing. And in any case, I am not a nice little girl. I'm an alien. Good morning to you."

I walked out of the police station, my back straight and my head held high. Little girls might run, skip, whistle and jump, but aliens, I felt certain, walked with dignity. With raised eyebrows, the guard watched me stride away. Then he shrugged his shoulders. "Odd creatures they are, to be sure, French people."

For the rest of the war, I went to the police station on the first Monday of every month. Each time I signed the book, I hoped to see the name of another alien living in Dungarvan. The war went on, and on, and on. And the only name ever to be seen in that nasty black book was my own, Sylvia Couturié.

Curraghmore, County Waterford, the ancestral home of the Marquesses of Waterford.

CHAPTER FOUR

Curraghmore

I N EARLY DECEMBER 1940, Lady Waterford wrote to
Wally saying that she would send her car the following
week to collect the three of us at eleven o'clock. Her chauffeur would take us to Curraghmore for lunch and would return us to Clonea Strand at four o'clock. Wearing our tight
and tidy clothes, the hems of our skirts having by now been
let down, we arrived shortly before twelve, driving down a
long avenue with rhododendrons growing in great shrubs
on both sides, and into a majestic courtyard. The car
stopped in front of the entrance and an extremely tall, dig-
nified looking butler appeared. After taking our coats in the
great hall, he led us into a drawing room where Lady Waterford gave us a warm welcome. We then went up to the
top floor of the very large house to the nursery where we
had lunch with Tyrone and Patrick, their Nanny and Wally.
After lunch we went for a walk in the garden and explored
a bizarre building the inside of which was covered with sea
shells. At four o'clock we were driven back to Clonea
Strand.

Petrol being strictly rationed from the very start of the
war, we repeated this visit only every three or four months.
We were always invited to stay for Easter and Christmas,
but Wally always refused for religious reasons. We became
very fond of Tyrone and Patrick as the years went by and always regretted not being able to stay longer with them, es-

pecially at Christmas when their older cousins the Daw-
nays, Millers and Girouards were there.

On that first Christmas night in Clonea Strand, under
my blanket in my narrow bed I sadly hummed and whistled
to myself the traditional French noels, *"Il est né le divin Enfant"*—The divine child is born—and *Les anges dans nos
campagnes"*—The angels in our countryside.

We never celebrated Christmas with Wally, except to
listen to the service and some carols on the wireless and
have perhaps better food and a piece of cake. It was a particularly sad day for us.

Clonea Strand was for Marguerite and me loneliness
and boredom. For two years we saw very few people. We
had no friends of our own age because we did not go to
school and there were no families near us, except during the
months of July and August when the other bungalows were
occupied. Our only neighbors were Mr. and Mrs. Maloney
at the edge of the tar road that ended at the beach. They
taught us to say in Irish such phrases as "How do you do?"
"Good morning," "Goodbye" and "God bless all here."

I didn't dare to knock often on their door. Johanna
Maloney appeared almost transparent, age seeming to have
dissolved her flesh. Sometimes, when she was in a good
mood, she let me sit beside the little peat fire while she
boiled her tea leaves in a saucepan and told me the legends
of her country. The old Celtic sagas were inhabited by a curious mixture of fairies, goblins and ghosts right along with
the saints and angels. There never were any devils, because
Saint Patrick had driven them away along with all the ser-
pents from green and Holy Ireland.

WE HAD TO BUY MILK AND EGGS so I went to the nearest farm twice a week, the milk can dangling from the
handlebars of my bicycle. I would ride across the field and
pedal up the steep climb that took me through the dark
wood on the other side of the road leading to Dungarvan. A

Lady Waterford with her sons Tyrone and Patrick, 1934.

Lady Waterford and Tyrone on horseback, 1941.

mile further on stood an old farmhouse with a thatched roof. The farmyard, compared to the ones I remembered in the Sarthe, was always disorderly and dirty. The farmer, Patrick Kennedy, was a man of about sixty years, though he looked far older. An only son, a rare thing in Ireland, rumor was that he was very rich. After having lived with his old mother until she died, he married a beautiful girl who was thirty years younger than himself. Every year young Mrs. Kennedy had a new baby. Her knowledge of cooking was limited and she was always too tired to clean her house. The Kennedy family lived on porridge, mutton stew, potatoes, cabbage, eggs and Jello. They drank a great deal of strong black tea. Mr. Kennedy also drank poteen, the raw illegal homemade Irish whisky. I always felt very sorry for tired, unhappy Mrs. Kennedy, especially as, with each new squealing baby, she lost more teeth. These were never thrown away but kept in a small tin. This collection she would produce and show proudly and sadly to everyone who came to the farm. She even showed me the holes in her mouth. An apple tree grew near the lane leading to the farmhouse. I always paid for the milk and eggs, but when they were ripe I would sometimes snitch an apple.

Simpleminded and a little frightening, because he would never look me in the face, but always stared at my chest and newly budding breasts, came Johnny McCarthy, every Saturday morning. In his donkey cart was a large milk can of fresh well water for drinking. Wally also bought firewood from him. As the logs were often too large, she bought a hatchet and a saw so that the wood could be cut and chopped to fit into the tiny stove and fireplace. Wood was very expensive, so Marguerite and I would comb the beach nearly every day in search of driftwood, which had to be dried before it was chopped. In good weather, Wally would also send us to pick up the cow dung in the field in front of the bungalow. Surprisingly, these dry cakes of dung did not have any unpleasant smell and they burned quite cheerfully.

"Driftwood and cow dung are gifts from God," Wally

said piously, because she did not pay for them as she did for wood and peat.

The postman came regularly with Wally's newspaper, *The Irish Independent*. My sister and I watched for the postman, hoping that one day he would bring not only the paper but a letter for us with news of our parents. Particularly at Christmas time or when we had a birthday, our hopes of receiving news, any news, mounted. Every evening we prayed earnestly, kneeling by the square brown table in the living room, for some scrap of news that our parents were still alive. But Christmas would come, our birthdays, Easter and the summer would come and go with our prayers unheeded.

Although the news in the paper was more or less a repetition of the BBC broadcasts of the previous day, I read all the war news carefully. The Battle of Britain raged on. The BBC was markedly more optimistic than the Irish newspaper which I thought sometimes made too much of Ireland's neutrality, always giving a favorable account of German successes. After reading the war news, I would study the weather forecast which also gave the time of high and low tides. This was important because of my shopping trips to Dungarvan. If the tide was low at the right time I could either go or come back part of the way on the beach, and this made the journey shorter.

Then I would turn to the obituaries, looking carefully at the photos of the people who had died. The notices fascinated me. The departed Irish had always been remarkably good. They were without fail "devoted" mothers or fathers; "faithful and loving" husbands or wives. One day, I thought, one of them will have lived a more exciting life and have done something really unusual—like swimming across the Atlantic or flying over a mountain with a kite—but no. These expressions of grief and sorrow "when the good Lord and the Blessed Virgin finally called" would always leave me wondering about the benefit which the living derived from publishing them.

"Do you think heaven is full of Irish people?" I asked

Wally one day. "Of course, all the Irish go to heaven," she answered. "What about the French?" I asked, thinking about my parents of whom we had had no news for over two years.

"I'm not sure; there's always some doubt about them."

"Oh my God," I thought. "I'm not sure that I ever want to go to heaven."

As time went by I felt it was more and more likely that our parents were dead, but I kept these dark thoughts strictly to myself and cut *The Irish Independent* into small squares to be used as lavatory paper.

By now Marguerite and I no longer spoke French to each other. I still often thought in French and sometimes dreamed in French that I was hunting in the forests of Touraine or learning a lesson at Jalesnes. But we now spoke English with an Irish brogue and this I thought was just as well, as there was really no reason to draw attention to ourselves.

The only French I said aloud, unbeknownst to Wally, was my nightly recitation in a precisely slow and well-articulated voice before going to sleep: *Le Corbeau et le Renard* (The Crow and the Fox, a classic French poem by La Fontaine), *Le Notre Père* (the Our Father), *Le Je Vous Salue Marie* (the Hail Mary).

The wireless which had been lent to us by Lady Susan Dawnay was installed on a shelf in a corner of the dark living room. It was powered with batteries that had to be bought and were very heavy and expensive. It was therefore a necessary economy to choose the programs with care. News bulletins were the priority, but Marguerite and I also listened in the evening to "Children's Hour," which we loved. It allowed us to escape for a short time from reports of air raids and battles and ramble in the realms of childhood and fairyland. The musical programs taught us the war songs, some of them new, many composed during the 1914–18 war and some from even earlier times. Brass regimental bands playing military music and the Scottish bagpipes were our favorites. We learned the various national anthems, and naturally "God Save Our King" and the "Marseillaise" were especially dear to us. The Belgian "La Brabançonne" appealed particularly to me, not only because of its rhythm but because it came from a small country of courageous men and women, and dear Mother Agnes.

For two reasons I took a great interest in the BBC's French bulletins and continually encouraged my sister to listen to them although she was not interested.

"We must not forget how to understand French," I would say to her, as she was fast forgetting all the French she knew, "even if we do not speak it any more."

For me, the announcer, Jean Oberlé, became and remained for several years my unique French teacher. He was my only link with France, its language and its way of thinking. It was an entirely one-sided conversation, but with a great master. Later, when little by little the French Resistance movement started to be organized, I listened to the mysterious messages and wondered to whom they were being sent. What did they mean? Who, for instance was the White Rabbit?

"Is the White Rabbit safe tonight?" I wondered. "What does Jean Oberlé look like?"

Many years later, I met both the White Rabbit and Jean Oberlé. I tried to tell them how much they had meant to a lonely girl living with her sister and governess between an Irish bog and the Atlantic Ocean, but I found it was too long, too sad, and too complicated to express, and so they never knew.

*F*INALLY, IN SEPTEMBER 1942, when I had almost given up all hope, the postman brought us a letter. It had been censored by the Swiss and the Germans, then the British and finally the Irish. It had been forwarded by the Red Cross, and came from Switzerland, written by our Decazes aunt, our father's sister, more than nine months earlier. I remembered this aunt quite well. She was tall, and often wore large floppy hats, pearl necklaces and a heavy gold bracelet. Hanging from the bracelet were gold medals on which were engraved the images of saints and the names of her children with the dates of their birth. She was a Duchess and we remembered that, when she came to Le Mesnil, she always brought us presents of delicious chocolate bars. When I was very small, I firmly believed that Switzerland was a country where chocolate trees grew.

The importance of this short first letter is almost impossible to express. Our aunt had received news of our parents. They were alive and well and at Le Mesnil. My aunt told us to write to her regularly, via the Red Cross, so that she could arrange to forward our news to our parents. Her hope was that we were continuing to be good children and enjoying ourselves in Ireland.

Marguerite and I were wildly happy. It didn't matter if the letter was nine months old and contained few details. For us it ended two long years of waiting. Our parents were not dead. They were alive. At least, nine months ago they were.

Marguerite danced around our tiny bungalow and sang a music hall lyric, *"Tout va très bien Madame la Marquise,"* her eyes shining with happiness.

The following day, though it was pouring rain, Wally was determined to ride her bicycle into Dungarvan. She was taking the letter, our letter, to show to her family and friends. It was plainly apparent that the good news was even more exciting to her because of who had written it. It greatly pleased the snob in her that our aunt was both a Duchess and a Catholic.

Very slowly, more letters began to filter through. Some came from Portugal where the Comtesse Armand, a friend of our parents, now lived. We were deeply grateful for every word, even though there was never much news because of the severe censorship. Several letters came from America where my mother had relatives. In 1943 a letter that particularly thrilled us came from our grandmother. She had es-

Our dear Aunt Maimaine, Duchesse Decazes, born Germaine Couturié.

caped from France and was now living with her sister in
California. Later the same year we were very excited to get
a long letter from our great-uncle Dick Tobin, our grandmother's brother. He had been American ambassador to
Holland and knew France very well. A correspondence
began and small gifts of pocket money and a few books arrived from time to time, though our American relatives
never realized in what poverty we were living.

One day an important looking letter arrived for Wally
from the American embassy in Dublin. At the request of
our American grandmother in California, an American
diplomat there had estimated that a woman and two children could live in Ireland on a certain sum of money and to
this effect had informed our American relatives, who
would now send us this amount twice a year through the
embassy. While pleased that at last regular family financial
help was on the way, Wally was furious about the amount
that had been quoted. "It's not enough to live on in the
slums of Limerick. We will barely survive on such a small
allowance," she said, "and what about my salary? I will
write again to Lord Derby."

It had also been strongly suggested that we should be
sent to a boarding school and the bills sent to America, or
that we ourselves be sent via Canada to our relatives there.
Both suggestions were firmly rejected by Wally.

She was our guardian "for the duration" and had a letter to prove it. We were her responsibility and hers alone.
Our relatives in the United States had never met Wally and
therefore had no idea of what her qualifications were. What
was important to Wally was that by maintaining the status
quo, she ensured her job and a regular stipend, however
paltry, which she could look forward to every six months. It
was undeniably true however, that crossing the Atlantic
was extremely dangerous. A Red Cross ship bound for
Canada with six hundred British children on board had already been sunk by a German submarine. "Wish me luck as
you wave me good-bye, Wish me luck as I go on my
way . . ." sang the children to their parents as the large

brightly lit Red Cross ship left Southampton, only to reach the bottom of the ocean. It was mid-winter and I listened to their singing on the radio. It was heartbreaking.

At fourteen, and having observed Wally at close quarters, I was now extremely suspicious of this mysterious "letter to prove it" that she so often invoked as the last word concerning her inviolate authority. I had never seen this document, and to my knowledge Wally had never shown it to anyone else. I was certain that my parents had not given her any such paper when they had come to Ireland for Christmas in 1939, since they had been firmly convinced at that time that we would return to France the following June. They had left us in the hands of the Ursuline nuns in Waterford, who were much better qualified than Wally to educate us. Had any such document arrived at Clonea Strand, Wally would surely have been only too happy to flourish it at the slightest provocation.

Oppressed by the thought that I was still too young to do anything about our situation and having learned to distrust adults, I could not decide on a course of action. I seriously considered going through Wally's private papers one day when she was in Dungarvan or visiting her family. Many things held me back. I wasn't certain that Marguerite would not tell her; I was most certain that Wally would beat me if she found me out; I was nagged by the thought of acting with disloyalty; I didn't know what my goal was, whether I found or failed to find something; and the top of her cupboard was always locked. Wally had decided to look after us when the Ursuline nuns had obliged us to leave their convent with no place to go, and now after two years nothing and no one was going to make her give us up. Perhaps in her strange way she had grown, if not fond of us, than inextricably involved. We were her job, and in wartime it wasn't a bad one. She had no one to question her, perhaps a little local prestige, enough money to eat and the prospect of more to come if our parents survived the war. And whether she valued our company or not, she was not alone and did not have to live with her family.

Beginning at the end of 1943, larger parcels began to arrive from California containing clothes. They were sent by our Aunt Sylvia, the wife of Uncle Richard, our mother's brother. Trying them on was exciting, but also a little sad because the bright Californian colors and light cottons were unsuitable to both Irish weather and Dungarvan style. And they were always too large for us.

"What big children our American cousins must be," I said, studying the garments to see in what way I could make them smaller. Of course, I couldn't change their vibrant colors. We only wore them under the dark, second-hand clothes that kind Irish people, whom we never met, gave to Wally for us. Still, these colorful garments gave us a secret pleasure and a sense of connection to a family that seemed now to grow less distant.

Wally was clever with her fingers and taught me how to knit and sew. By the time I was fourteen, I was altering my own clothes and knitting sweaters and socks for the winter. Undoing old knitted sweaters, I would re-use the different colored wool to knit new ones with Fair Isle designs. After a while I became quite good at knitting and managed to read a book at the same time.

One problem was our feet. They never looked any larger, but the shoes continued to shrink. Wally at last bought me a pair of sandals, insisting that they be several sizes too large so that they would last a long time. Marguerite wore my old ones. The sandals were uncomfortable and remained in the porch. If someone arrived, we would rapidly put them on; otherwise we went barefoot except when we went to Curraghmore or Dungarvan.

Wally wrote regularly to our American relatives, making a point of telling them how fond of us she was and including glowing reports of how well she was continuing our education. The letters I wrote myself were carefully scrutinized. I think perhaps Wally's censorship was one of the strictest of the war. I was to have only the nicest things to say about her, and I had to lay it on a little thick about how happy we were in Ireland. Any letter containing even a mild complaint had to be rewritten.

"How dare you be disloyal to me," she would say, rereading every word in search of the slightest sign of what she considered a criticism. She did not reciprocate with the letters she wrote herself, the contents of which were a mystery to me. Nor was I always shown the letters she received from them. She never made Marguerite write a letter, though my sister would sometimes add a few words at the bottom of mine.

As for letters from France, the fact that our parents were living north of the Loire River, under German occupation, made things more difficult. In the southern part of the country, administered by the Vichy Government, conditions were easier. Over two and a half years elapsed before a six-month-old letter in our mother's elegant handwriting arrived. After that we received two or three letters a year. They came by way of Switzerland or Portugal and always through the Red Cross. They were strictly censored and she always said the same thing.

"Daddy and I are well, we hope that you are well and having a lovely time. Tommy and Dots, your ponies, are well and we all send our love. Your Mummy."

The thought of our ponies sending their love was ludicrous. I was longing for news of everyone at Le Mesnil, particularly of my cousins Colette, Myriam and Rose. I was worried about what had happened to them, whether they were alive or dead. I realized that my mother thought that we were still little children, but it was odd to me that she did not look at other girls my age in France to visualize how I had grown, did not listen to them to discover what my interests might be. Perhaps she wrote that way because of the censorship, though our Aunt Maimaine in Switzerland did not. I wondered what was wrong with her, her letters were so empty. However, even if these letters were disappointing, at least they were proof that we were not orphans. At least not for the time being.

ONE DAY AS I WAS PICKING UP OUR MEAT RATION at the door of the butcher's shop, Mrs. Flynn asked, "What do you do with yourself all day, dearie, out on that lonely Clonea Strand?"

I explained that there was a lot to do, finding and chopping wood, getting the milk, cleaning the bungalow, sewing, and Wally's lessons with pages of poems to learn, not to mention long walks on the beach which Wally said were good for our health.

"You must miss your parents." said Mrs. Flynn.

"Yes, very much," I answered.

"Now, what else would you be missing most out there?"

"Books," was my unhesitating reply.

Mrs. Flynn thought for a moment, then said, "That's not difficult. You go down Main Street, dearie, and on your right, you'll find a lending library. Miss Mary and Miss Rita Clancy look after it. Here's sixpence so that you can borrow your first book."

By now I was making no fuss about taking pennies from kind Mrs. Flynn.

"Thank you very much, and may God bless you," I added politely.

The Dungarvan lending library was a small and dusty place. Peering through owl-like spectacles, Miss Mary Clancy greeted me kindly. She was a small thin woman who often dressed in pink, with many frills and bows. She found a book for me, explaining that it should be returned the following week or exchanged on payment of another sixpence for a different one.

I decided that it was wiser not to tell Wally about the lending library. I covered the book with the jacket of *Lorna Doone,* which she had gotten for me at Christmas, and proceeded to discover the fascinating world of Jane Austen and the Brontës under her unsuspecting nose.

At this point, however, a new problem arose. Wally had decided that our lamp would be extinguished after the nine o'clock news. This didn't suit me because I had to stop reading. Bedroom doors were left open throughout the night for warmth, which meant that Wally could see if a candle was lit in my room. After serious consideration, I decided that reading by torch light was the best idea.

At Christmas, uncle Dick Tobin in America had sent us a little pocket money. Wally had taken some of it "for the house" but she didn't dare take it all. I had saved a pound note and I took it with me the next time I went to Dungarvan. After the weekly shopping, I went to the hardware store and bought a small flat torch and two batteries from Mr. Siberry.

Next I went to the library. Miss Clancy asked, "Do you want one or two books?"

"How many am I allowed to have each week?"

"You can have two."

"Fine, I'll take two every week, but they must be small because I have to carry them back to Clonea Strand on my bicycle with our shopping."

"Oh, so you're one of the French girls. You don't look very French. I always thought they had dark eyes and hair."

"Yes, I'm French," I replied politely. I was now in the habit of giving very little information about myself.

"Well, in that case, I'll only ask you to pay for half of the books you borrow."

"Oh, thank you very much. You are very kind. I'll be very careful not to damage them." She was a very charming Dungarvan person, I thought.

From that day forward, with the help of the two Miss Clancys and the flashlight that enabled me to read in bed, I read two books a week until I had read all the books in the Dungarvan lending library, some of them several times.

At last spring arrived in Clonea Strand and I started bathing in the ocean. Our long winter solitude had made us very shy. I at least escaped once a week to Dungarvan, on a hard ten-mile bicycle ride to do the shopping, but for two years Marguerite's world consisted of Wally, the postman and me.

In March, I wrote to Uncle Dick in America saying that I would very much like to learn how to play tennis. There was a court in front of the Ocean View Hotel where I could play. Uncle Dick sent me money to buy a tennis racket, balls and shoes. I chose these carefully in a Dungarvan shop. I also bought two yards of white cotton to make a skirt. Sitting on the stone fence in front of the bungalow, I sewed the skirt, and when it was finished, I was fully equipped for my first game.

"Come with me, Marguerite, it's going to be fun." She carried the two tennis balls and off we went.

Setting out from the bungalow dressed all in white, I was aware that I was looking unusually tidy. I felt well and happy.

My skirt, which I had made, and the white blouse, which had come from America and which I had cut down to my size, were giving me more pleasure than any clothes I had ever worn. It was partly because I had made them myself and partly because the right clothes are important in any sport. I had always worn jodhpurs when I rode my pony. By wearing white, I was not only conforming to my distant parents' expectations but also overcoming my shyness, gaining confidence from the knowledge of my correct appearance. I did not doubt that, having gone to so much trouble to look right, I would immediately be invited to play.

On the beach, I began to swing my racket in imitation of people I had seen playing. Marguerite and I ran and danced on the sand in anticipation of the pleasure to come.

We were flushed and out of breath as we shyly entered the tennis court and sat down to watch the mixed doubles game that was already in progress. Other people arrived and replaced the original players. I stayed on, hoping that someone would ask me to play, even if it was only to hit a few balls, but no. As the afternoon drew to a close, it became colder and the sun disappeared. We sat in a huddle. I was far too shy to ask if I could play or pick up stray balls, and no one bothered to ask me what I was doing, all dressed up in white.

We walked back to Sunnyside in silence with heavy hearts. I had a choking sensation in my throat. No one had even said hello.

"Never mind," whispered my sister. "Next year, I will be bigger and you will ask uncle Dick to send me money so that we can play together."

"Maybe . . . maybe."

It was a sad, melancholy Saturday. I thought of home, of parents, of cousins, and decided I had not grown up at all.

The following year I had better luck, and after hours of picking up other people's tennis balls I was sometimes invited to play. A kind man taught me how to serve and swing the racquet properly. I loved playing tennis because it completely took my mind off the war. I remember a girl named Marion Malloney, who asked me to play quite often. It was a small thing, but it connected me to another person at a time when I was cut off from human kindness, and I was very grateful.

With the arrival of the summer holidays and warmer weather, the other bungalows were occupied by families who came to spend a few weeks by the sea. Most of them owned small shops of various kinds in Clonmel just beyond the mountains, not very far away by car. To us it meant children of our own age playing on the beach. Screwing up our courage, Marguerite and I talked to them, bathed with them and found them friendly. The less we became like our former selves, the less strange we appeared to them.

Unfortunately, this camaraderie did not last long. Wally arrived on the beach one afternoon, watched the happy scene for a moment, then, looking very grim, walked back to our bungalow, slamming the door behind her. When we returned in the evening, chatting happily together about our new friends, Wally closed the front door and the windows.

My uncle Richard Raoul-Duval, with his wife, our Aunt Sylvia, and their children, our cousins Diane, Joan and Michael, in California, 1944.

Marguerite and me with our American tennis rackets. I am no longer wearing white and my sister is without shoes.

"You must stop playing with those children," she shouted. "You must only say good morning and good evening and you must never go into any of the other bungalows. Those people are of a different class; they are shopkeepers. How dare you forget who you are. You should always remember that you have an aunt who is a Duchess. I will keep a close eye on you both this summer, and in any case I will be giving you extra lessons from now on."

She kept her word and saw to it that we never played with the Irish shopkeepers' children that summer. It was a particularly cruel thing to do to us, so desperate were we for human contact. It was not healthy and we retreated further into our timidity and sadness.

That night before going to sleep I said to myself "Wally is a fool. When I grow up I will not divide people this way." I went to sleep dreaming of the friends I would have, from widely varying backgrounds and every corner of the earth, someday.

Marguerite and me, gazing out to sea and thinking of home.

CHAPTER FIVE

A Trifle Pudding

A SUMMER ATTRACTION AT CLONEA STRAND was the
dance held at the hotel every Saturday evening. Reading very late into the night, I could hear from across the
small living room the regular sound of loud snoring which
meant that Wally was fast asleep. Marguerite, poor thing,
had to bear the brunt of it. Her bed was only a yard away
from Wally's and I was very thankful not to have to share a
room. My room was small, but at least I was alone and had
a measure of privacy. My window was open and from a distance I could clearly hear the sound of Irish music that I remembered so well from our first summer near Cork. I
started to move my feet under my blanket in time with the
music and let my mind drift with the melodies. What was it
like over there, I wondered?

Handsome lads dancing with the dark-haired, green-eyed Irish colleens. The hall would be filled with light and
music. There must be laughter. How I wished I could join in
the jigs, the reels and the hornpipes.

One Saturday night, I did not undress completely but
went to bed and read, waiting for Wally to snore. Then,
making as little noise as possible, I put a warm navy blue
sweater over my cotton dress. I slipped on my sandals because I was frightened of snakes and unable to fully believe
that St. Patrick had chased every last one from Holy Ireland.
Even a saint could have missed a few in the bog.

Gingerly, holding my breath, I climbed over the window sill, crossed our tiny garden and climbed over the wall into the dark night. My heart pounding, I ran across the moonlit field to the dark bog, the only safe path if I didn't want to be seen. Most people were too frightened by the proximity of moving sands to cross it at night, and they took long detours. Intimately familiar with the landscape in my remote corner of the world, I did not fear them. I crossed quickly, with sure steps, into the adjacent field where cattle grazed. Here I walked slowly to be sure not to frighten the old bull and his cows. I knew that they would not hurt me. I was convinced that animals never attack children unless they are frightened or hungry.

A high hedge loomed up and the shadow it cast was also a protection. Slowly, more carefully now, I walked on tiptoe to the low shed that stood against the wall at the back of the hotel. Up on to the roof of the shed I climbed. From there I could look through a small window into the dance hall. I watched for a long time, lying flat on my tummy with my chin in my hands. People were laughing, dancing and having fun. Later I turned away, and lying on my back under the starlit sky, gave myself up completely to the lovely sounds of the Irish music.

It was a magical sound, I thought, beating time with my fingers happily and humming the tunes. The music stopped for a few minutes while the musicians rested and had a drink. As I lay motionless in the silence of the night, I listened to the quiet voice of my heart. "Music is free," it said. "Music belongs to everyone. You only have to listen." Some knowledge is full of bliss.

I was to enjoy several of these escapades on Saturday nights that summer, but I never entered the dance hall. No, if Wally ever found out, I thought she would surely kill me.

When the dance was nearly over, I let myself carefully drop from the roof of the shed on to the grass. Peering catlike into the darkness, I was careful not to bump into any blooming lovers who might recognize me and tell Wally. The beach way was shorter but that was where I knew loving couples sat, holding hands and kissing. So I always danced my way back to the bungalow through my dark mysterious bog, telling myself that one night if I was lucky I might meet fairies in long green dresses or other Little People. They to be sure would catch my hand, claim me as one of their own and together we would dance on the moonbeams right up to the stars.

SHORTLY BEFORE CHRISTMAS, Lady Waterford sent her chauffeur to Clonea Strand to bring Marguerite, Wally and me to Curraghmore for lunch and to spend the afternoon. Tyrone and Patrick played mostly with my sister who was closer to their age. Fortunately for me, their older cousins were also there. Blanche Dawnay, Lady Susan Dawnay's granddaughter, became my best friend that afternoon, my only friend. She was a cheerful girl and I admired her.

"I want to go to school with Blanche," I said several times, but no flame of enthusiasm was ever kindled in Wally's heart by my pleas.

"That is quite impossible. First of all, the school is far too expensive and secondly, it is Protestant." The first obstacle might have been surmounted; the second, never.

That day Blanche's twin brothers Hugh and Peter were also there. About eight years old, they had round pink faces and brown eyes. They were real little devils. As we went out to play after lunch, Hugh kicked my ankle and I promptly kicked him back, calling him *"cochon."* Instead of running away he stopped in front of me and, looking me straight in the eye, asked me what *cochon* meant and was it an insult?

"Yes, it's an insult and it means 'pig' in French." To my surprise he said "thank you" and then walked away, repeating *"cochon . . . cochon."* He never forgot it and it was his first word in a foreign language.

The delightful setting at Curraghmore continued to captivate me. I loved the wide alleys and lawns surrounding the imposing eighteenth century house. Marguerite and I enjoyed our visits to this beautiful place and they broke the monotony of Clonea Strand. Unfortunately, they were rare because of petrol rationing. The nursery on the top floor was an ideal area for games of hide and seek because of its maze of corridors, large and small rooms, wide and narrow stairs. The drawing rooms and the dining room were full of light thanks to the tall windows, and large fires burned there in winter. Lovely paintings, mostly portraits, hung on the walls. Curraghmore was a cheerful house, seemingly forever filled with people and their friendly dogs.

We were always called down to the drawing room before tea to say "How do you do" to the grown-ups. While we children were playing, Wally sat with the other nannies and governesses, rapt in gossipy conversation.

One day she told us that she had heard that Curraghmore was haunted and that the ghost of a greyhound could be seen walking around the house and garden when a member of the family had recently died or was about to. This seemed odd because although there were several dogs of different breeds in the house, there was not a single greyhound. One evening, after a visit, Wally told us that the ghostly greyhound had been seen by the servants. Marguerite was worried but I was skeptical and did not believe her story. However, when we returned to Curraghmore a few months later, Tyrone and Patrick told us that one of their uncles had been killed fighting the Germans in a big sea battle. Both little boys were very sad.

"He was our favorite uncle," said Tyrone. "Our father died when we were little and we can't remember him. This makes our uncles very important to us. I hope the Germans won't kill the others, too."

We both were wide-eyed with sympathy and felt that it was not the appropriate moment to ask about the greyhound ghost.

The Duchess of St. Albans, Tyrone and Patrick's grandmother, had a long talk with me after lunch at Curraghmore one day. Finding out about my longing to learn how to play the piano, she said she had one not in use, in Newtown

Lady Susan Dawnay
with her grandchildren
Patrick and Romayne.

The Dawnay family:
Rachel, Hugh, Lady
Katherine, Peter and
Blanche.

Anna, the Irish estate of the Duke of St. Albans, and would send it down to Clonea Strand "for the duration."

She also discovered that I was very worried because I was forgetting how to speak French. To cheer me up, she told me that she would send two French books to me every month which, after reading, I must return and two more would be forwarded. When the first French books arrived, Wally looked at them. She had no desire to read them herself and in fact never read any book even in English.

Carefully rewrapping the books in the same thick brown paper they had come in, she put them on top of her wardrobe and said, "No, you are not going to read these books. I won't let you have your mind corrupted by dirty French books or by a Protestant, even if she is a Duchess." Her voice filled with that strange mix of menace and pleasure she always got when she felt she was defending her God.

An explanation, I felt, to Tyrone's kind grandmother was both urgent and necessary. I decided to ask his help on our next visit to Curraghmore.

"Tyrone, I want to tell you a secret and you must help me, please," I whispered.

Feeling happy and important that a girl who was three years older should want to confide in him and need his help, he whispered back, "Follow me. We will go to the rose garden which is a very good place for telling secrets. The gardener is probably tending the vegetables."

"I want to show Sylvia my new pony," Tyrone told his nanny as we left the house together. He was a good looking little boy, with a high forehead, blue eyes, pink cheeks and fair hair. He was always dressed in gray flannel trousers and hand-knitted sweaters.

Out of the house we ran, going first to the stables where a quick inspection for truth's sake was made of the new pony, and then on to the rose garden, well protected from the wind by a stone wall. As he had said it would be, the garden was deserted.

"Listen carefully," I began. "A week after our last visit to Curraghmore, your grandmother sent me two French books. I wasn't allowed to read them. Wally took them away from me and sent them back. First of all she said that French books are always dirty—I suppose she meant immoral. Then she gave another reason, that your grandmother is a Protestant." I stamped my foot furiously as I said these words.

"Anyhow, I want you to tell your grandmother not to send any more. Don't tell her why; she will guess the reason. You must swear to me that you won't tell another soul. If this gets back to Wally, as sure as hell she will kill me."

Tyrone promised under oath, crossing his throat with a rather grubby finger, that he would pass on the message to his Granny and not tell another soul. "Or may I drop dead," he added solemnly. He was a very responsible and sensitive little boy and I knew my secret would be quite safe with him. No other French books ever found their way to Clonea Strand. Sometime later, however, an old piano arrived, and Wally did not dare send it back. I wrote a very grateful letter to the Duchess of St. Albans.

That night we heard on the wireless of the sinking of the French fleet by its own naval officers at Toulon. I was both proud that the Germans had not been able to steal our warships and ashamed that all the officers had not escaped with their ships to North Africa, as two of them had successfully done.

THERE WERE SEVERAL BAD STORMS that winter and a number of sea mines were washed up on our beach. I immediately rode my bicycle into Dungarvan to tell the guards. I admired the brave man who dismantled them. Three times I saw a mine out at sea hit a rock, exploding with an enormous bang and sending water high up into the sky. We also heard of a drowned sailor found on a neighboring beach.

At Easter that year Wally's sister Madge sent Marguerite a puppy, a white Maltese terrier. Marguerite called her Biddy. She slept on Marguerite's bed and provided her with doggy warmth and comfort.

As time went by, Wally would often shake her head and talk to us about our future.

"Even if your parents survive the war, you will have to work for your living. If they are killed, you will have to work even harder," she said, her eyes boring into us to make her point.

"I want to be an explorer," I told her.

"That," Wally answered, "is not a woman's job. You had better study your spelling and become a secretary. If the worst comes, you could be a chambermaid in one of the grand Irish mansions. French maids are much appreciated in Ireland."

The prospect of life as a French chambermaid was not very interesting to me. I already knew that I did not like housework. I thought that I had better start learning how to become a good secretary as soon as possible.

The next time I went to Dungarvan, I had a talk with my friend, Mrs. Flynn.

"Mrs. Flynn, please, I want to learn how to become a good secretary. What is the best way?"

"That's an easy one," she answered. "Now, you just go along to the Dungarvan Technical School. They turn out secretaries. They teach typing and shorthand. It's a ways down that street on the right of the square."

"Is it . . . is it frightfully expensive?"

"Oh, no dear. It's a state school and practically free. Although you will have to buy some books."

"Thank you, Mrs. Flynn, and may God bless you," I said with a happy smile, and down the street I went to the Dungarvan Technical School. I looked at the big, modern box of a building for a long time. Summoning up all my courage, I walked slowly up the steps and into the hall. A woman was sitting behind a desk.

"How do you do. What do you want?" she asked me.

"I have come to find out how and when I can enroll in this school. I want to become a secretary."

"It's February now, and the school year starts in September, and first of all, you must be fourteen."

"I'm nearly fourteen."

"You don't look that old; you look barely twelve. Where are you going to school now?"

"I'm not going to school. I'm French and live out on Clonea Strand with my sister and Miss Walsh, our governess. She is educating us."

"But Clonea Strand is five miles away. How on earth do you think that you are going to be able to get here? Ten miles a day, five days a week, is a long way for a small girl like you."

"Oh, no, I would do it with pleasure. I am small and skinny but I'm never ill and I'm strong as a mountain goat. In any case, for two years now I have been coming to Dungarvan once or twice a week to do our shopping, so two or three more days won't hurt me."

There was a long silence.

"All right," said the lady. "When will you be fourteen?"

"Next month."

"Well, as you are in such a hurry, talk to your governess, bring me your passport and I will make an exception. You can start next Monday."

I whistled and sang Irish melodies and the "Marseillaise" all along the road and over the crooked bridge back to Clonea Strand. I hoped that Wally would agree to the secretarial course at the Technical School. After all, it was her idea that I should become a secretary, and yet, as usual, I was worried.

Wally, to my surprise, said yes. To be able to go to school at last. It was bliss. I would work very hard, I promised myself. I might even be a credit to Wally. The company of boys and girls of my own age alone was enough to drive me to succeed. Wally presented herself at the school office and paid the small fee and the cost of the books. At the Devonshire Arms Hotel, the only hotel in Dungarvan, she arranged for me to have lunch five days a week at a table, by myself, in a corner of the dining room, slightly apart from

Dungarvan Technical School.

Mai Flaherty and me
several years later at Le
Mesnil, after my return
from the French delegation
to the United Nations
in New York.

the traveling salesmen and the farmers who, on market days, crowded the place. Some men kept their tweed caps on their heads while eating, and this intrigued me. Peeking from behind my ever-present book, I watched with interest their chewing faces.

The menu at the Devonshire Arms was a perfect monument to consistency. There was essentially one meal, with little variation. It was composed of a small piece of mysterious meat, cabbage, two kinds of boiled potatoes, white and yellow, and some days turnips or parsnips, with jelly or an apple for desert. I drank water and strong black tea. The service was slow.

After the first week, I paid Wally a compliment telling her that her meals at Sunnyside were better than those at the hotel. Wally enjoyed cooking. Our meager ingredients never varied, but her preparations often did. She was proud of her skill, and my appreciation pleased her immensely, and so generous was I in my newfound freedom, I was happy to see her smile.

The students at the Technical School were very friendly and I found them kinder and more straightforward than the girls at the Waterford convent. Perhaps this was due to the fact that by now I had completely lost my French accent and spoke with a southern Irish brogue, repeating the locally ingrained grammatical errors.

Soon a girl called Mai Flaherty became my friend. She looked more Spanish than Irish. She had soft brown eyes, a large generous mouth that turned up at the corners and a dimple in the middle of her chin. What I liked about her was that she was good humored, intelligent and hardworking. She was the best student in our class, generous and perceptive, and somehow understood things without asking indiscreet questions. She sort of adopted me, the stranger, and became my protector. We loved being together and she became my best friend in Dungarvan.

The secretarial course lasted two years and consisted of accounting, English, Gregg shorthand, typewriting, and— once a week—either sewing or cooking. It was not very dif-

ficult. But just as important as the lessons was simply read-
justing to being around other people.

WALLY HAD A SWEET TOOTH, loved to eat and suffered
more than we did from the rationing. She had a particular weakness for cakes and desserts, and whenever possible made one as a great treat. First she would install
Marguerite by the kitchen table and would get her to sift
flour into a bowl through an old silk stocking. There were
mysterious particles in the dark wartime flour and these
would be carefully sifted out, remaining caught in the stocking. With the small amount of clean white flour in the bowl,
Wally would set to work. First she made our bread with sour
milk and baking soda. Then, if there was enough flour left,
she would add a little sugar and an egg or egg powder and
some margarine to make some kind of pudding or cake.

Shortly after I had started attending the Technical
School, Wally made a trifle pudding for Sunday lunch. It
was a great success. We ate half immediately and then Wally
put the remainder into the cupboard, saying that we would
finish it for supper.

As it was a fine day, she decided to bicycle into Dungarvan to visit a friend for the afternoon. Before leaving, she
gave Marguerite poetry to learn and sums to do. She then
told me that Johnny Maloney had said we could use a small
section of his vegetable plot. He would continue to sell us
potatoes but was unable to supply anything more. The
arrangement therefore was that we would grow our own
vegetables on the piece of ground he rented to us.

"Johnny is expecting you," Wally said to me. "He will
show you the plot, lend you a spade, and show you how to
use it. Start preparing the soil and next week you can sow
some carrots and radishes."

I loved working out-of-doors. The small piece of land
was situated between a narrow stream and a high wall. The
soil was rich and there were a lot of weeds. After I had

pulled these out I started to dig the soft earth. Being an inexperienced gardener, I found the work tiring and soon I was exhausted. My legs were very strong but my shoulders and my arms were not. Traveling ten miles a day in every kind of weather, even though I was reluctant to admit it, was sapping my strength. My mornings started at six cleaning the fireplace and the stove and setting them with newspaper and kindling wood so that Wally would only have to put a match to them when she and Marguerite got up later. I would then make myself a cup of tea on the primus, wash my face and hands in cold rainwater, quickly dress and ride off to school with two or three cold boiled potatoes in my pocket. Sometimes, if I woke earlier, I would heat a bowl of porridge, but I seldom had time and, in any case, I liked the boiled potatoes. Porridge became a Saturday or Sunday morning treat.

Looking at my afternoon's work in the garden, I thought that Wally would be satisfied with what I had done and decided to return to the bungalow. I found it empty. Marguerite must have gone to play or look for driftwood on the beach. I took off my rubber boots, which I wore without socks but lined with paper soles cut out of *The Irish Independent*. I went to my room, climbed under the blanket on my bed and fell asleep immediately. Some time later Wally's voice wakened me. Before I even opened my eyes I knew she was in a towering temper.

"Come here," she yelled at the top of her voice. "Come here at once, Sylvia!" Wondering what on earth had happened, I obeyed. Wally was trembling with uncontrollable rage.

"You are a thief and a greedy pig. You have helped yourself to the trifle and it's practically all gone."

"Dear God," I thought, trying hard not to lose my own temper. Then in a low, quiet voice, as soon as Wally stopped for breath, I said, "Wally, I have not eaten any trifle since lunch time. I went straight to work in the garden. When I came back, I didn't even go into the kitchen. I went straight to my room and have been sleeping ever since."

Wally's voice, low and threatening, hissed, "So not

only are you a thief and a greedy pig, but you are also a liar. My duty is to give you the beating of your life. I will beat you black and blue."

As she began to take off her horrid leather belt, I ran into my room and bolted the door. Quickly, I closed the window. When Wally began pounding on the door, I pushed my table against it.

"How dare you, how dare you, you filthy bastard!" I looked into the water jug, reassured myself that it was full, and said to Wally, "I won't come out of this room until you take back all you have said. I am not a greedy pig. I am not a thief and I am not a liar. It's a dead girl you are going to have on your hands if you don't look out."

"Come out at once," Wally shouted back. "In any case, you have nothing to eat in your room. You'll have to come out sooner or later."

"There are things more important than eating. I don't mind if I die."

Wally answered that she didn't care either. Later I heard her in the kitchen making tea and guessed that she and Marguerite were finishing the trifle pudding for their supper.

The first day went fairly well. I was too upset to be hungry. Fortunately, there were a few sweets hidden on top of my cupboard. The narrow room had rough, unpainted walls. The metal bed was high and a chest of drawers stood against the wall. A small table covered with an oilcloth held an enamel basin and tall jug full of water. Under this table was a blue enamel pail with a cover that I used as a toilet. On the door of the cupboard where my coat and dresses hung, a narrow mirror was fixed. The table that I normally used when studying stayed pushed against the door. A supply of matches and candles were always hidden in my room, as were my library books and my electric torch.

The second day was far from pleasant. Luckily, I also had my schoolbooks. I studied my shorthand lessons, doing each exercise over and over. I tried not to think of food and went to bed early, pushing my stomach in with both my fists. The third day, I was beginning to feel weak, but wild horses would not make me give in now. I drank a lot of water. It was in the late afternoon of the fourth day that Wally finally gave in. Her voice was calm. "Come out of that room right away," she said. "I will give you your own way. You are a very bad girl, and I hate to think what will happen to you later in life, but you are not a liar."

"Or a thief?" I asked.

"Or a thief."

With great relief, I unlocked my door and stepped into the living room. Wally was a heavy woman, but she was very strong and quick in her movements when she wanted. I was totally unsuspecting and I had no time to protect myself before Wally was on me, slapping me with all her strength, giving vent to the rage that she had been building for four days. Left, right, left, right, the heavy hands hit my face, my head, my neck. The beating went on and on. It only stopped once I had fallen to the floor, no longer having the strength to defend myself. She gave me a kick.

"That will teach you never to lie again," she huffed as she went into the kitchen to make herself a cup of tea and smoke a cigarette.

Slowly, I opened my eyes and looked around the already darkening living room. In the far corner, hiding between the cupboard and the wall, making herself as scarce as possible, was Marguerite. She looked like a small, frightened animal. Her eyes were red and looked strangely both anguished and pleading.

"So that's the story," I thought, understanding finally penetrating my ringing head. "You poor little thing. You ate the trifle. I thought that Wally had miscalculated what was left, but she had not made a mistake."

Marguerite had eaten the trifle because she was hungry and then, when she had seen Wally's rage, she had been too frightened to confess. Poor child, she must have been even more miserable than I was during those last four days. "Don't be frightened any more," my eyes said to my sister. "I understand. I won't give you away to the old witch. There's no point in both of us getting a beating."

I returned to my bedroom, opened the window, then went outside and filled the water jug. Half filling the basin, I placed it on the floor, lay on the cold linoleum and plunged my face and head into the cool rainwater. I remained very still for several minutes, only turning my head from side to side. It did not matter if my hair was wet and sticking to my head. It would dry. The cold water was already numbing the pain. I didn't hear my sister tiptoeing into the room.

"Are you all right?" she whispered.

"I'll be all right. Don't worry."

"Thank you for not giving me away."

"It's not important. Forget about it. But don't ever again let someone else take a punishing in your place. It's too unfair."

"Thank you," she said, quietly retreating to her dark corner.

After a while, I felt less pain. I gently wiped my face with a towel, then turned to look at myself in the mirror.

"Good God. Oh, I do look awful." My face was both red and white. One eye was about twice its usual size, the other I could barely open. Large dark circles underlined them and across my face and neck there were the marks of Wally's heavy fingers. "What a mess," I said to myself.

Dazed from the lack of food and the beating, I began to talk to my mirror in search of comfort.

"Mirror, mirror, tell me true, do you ever tell a lie?"

"Yes," lied the mirror.

This made me smile and the funny face that looked only a little like my own smiled back.

The sound of Wally's voice cut across this dreamy dialogue and brought me back to reality.

"Sylvia, Sylvia, come in here straight away."

Feeling miserable, I walked slowly into the kitchen. Wally inspected me closely.

"Your face looks awful," she said. "You won't be able to go to school for at least a week."

"Why not? I don't mind going back tomorrow. I'll be all right by then," I said, bravely.

"Not with that face you won't, my girl. You will stay right here until you look normal again and when you do go back, you will tell your teacher that you have had a bad cold with a temperature and were unable to leave the house."

"Yes, Wally," came the no longer protesting answer. Wally was very pleased to have won her battle. She gave me a cup of tea and a piece of freshly baked soda bread.

That evening, as every evening, we said our prayers together. We first said the Rosary, then the evening prayers which always ended with Marguerite and me saying: "God bless our father and mother and grandmother and keep them safe. God bless Wally who is so good and kind to us and keep her well." Then together we would all say "Amen."

On my return to school the following week, I gave Miss Patterson a detailed description of my cold. She was glad to see me back and pleased that I had studied some shorthand at home, as the class had now reached page ninety-eight. I said that I thought I could catch up, and did not tell her that I had completed all the exercises in the book. I had known how to keep silent for years, but this was something entirely different. Now I had lied for the first time in my life, under adult instruction. It had worked, and caused no pain. From that time on, whenever I was late coming back from Dungarvan, I would let the air out of one tire of my bicycle as I was nearing the bungalow and walk the last hundred yards. Wally then, instead of scolding and punishing me for being late, would be quite kind and would allow me to mend my bike for the next day instead of making me wash the dishes. It was a useful trick and I used it often.

When the weather was fine, Marguerite would wait for my return from school, sitting on the stone wall of the garden. She would always make me think of William Wordsworth's sad poem,

> No mate, no comrade, Lucy knew;
> She dwelt on a wide moor
> The sweetest thing that ever grew
> Beside a cottage door.

Me looking out to sea in 1940, looking toward France and longing to go hom

CHAPTER SIX

The Storm

*A*T LAST, IT WAS SPRING AGAIN. The ever blowing wind had decided to have a rest. The wildflowers growing in the hedges could stand straight, quietly looking around, nodding to each other. Let the wind rest. Let the wildflowers, sweet smelling herbs, the grass, the leaves and birds be free to enjoy the calm evening hour.

I was whistling a happy little tune, cycling home from school along the narrow winding road, over the ancient crooked stone bridge where sometimes I stopped to rest, absently memorizing shorthand characters and wondering if anybody could write 120 words a minute and if so, who would actually dictate 120 words of sense a minute? Why such haste? On this particular evening, the answer did not seem important. Better by far listen to the birds, watching out for that funny little fellow with the distinctive cry "A-little-piece-of-bread-and-no-cheese, A-little-piece-of-bread-and-no-cheese." What was his name? I could not remember for certain, and thought that it perhaps was a nightingale.

Still no wind. Just one more mile to Clonea Strand and hot tea, the BBC and Jean Oberlé. An evening when all is well. I had learned to enjoy the moment. "No problems today," I thought. The war, constantly in the back of my mind, seemed very far away now. Africa, Tripoli, Bir Hakeim—nothing I could do about it. Some days were like that. Other days the war seemed about to explode just over our heads.

The weeks and months dragged on. To my sister and me it seemed that the war would never end. Time moved slowly. Would we ever see our home again? That summer I often stood at night on the edge of the sea, looking up at the maze of stars, looking and dreaming.

By 1943, several people had discovered where we lived and had written to Wally saying that they were friends of our parents. One letter came from Lady Granard, an American living north of Dublin, a friend of our grandmother's. She invited us to stay with her for a holiday or, if we wished, until the end of the war. Her house, Castle Forbes, was large, she said, and she would happily welcome us. Wally thanked her but refused, saying that we would stay at Clonea Strand.

Lady Granard sent presents of money and books and at Christmas time two small alarm clocks. We were never allowed to visit her. Wally as always had a ready excuse: "She lives too close to Northern Ireland."

At about the same time, Mrs. Scrope wrote from Yorkshire, explaining that she had been to the same boarding school as our mother and was a friend. She had often stayed at Le Mesnil. She was a Catholic with six children and did not mind in the least having two more. If we did come to stay, she would send us to the school her own daughter Sally attended and consequently would not require Wally's services. This letter was very badly received.

HOW DARE SHE PRESUME SUCH A THING. I am your guardian for the duration. Yorkshire is dangerous, and in any case, I don't remember having met this woman. Mrs. Scrope, indeed! She doesn't even have a title," she sniffed.

What Wally didn't know was that even without a title, the Scrope family was one of the oldest in England. One

Scrope was a character in Shakespeare's *Henry V.* Her maiden name was among the grandest in Yorkshire. But this sort of subtlety was beyond Wally, for all her snobbishness, and some very disagreeable letters were exchanged between them. Our lives remained unchanged. I was more and more fed up with our situation, but on we stayed at Clonea Strand.

*A*NYONE WHO HAS LIVED by the Atlantic Ocean knows that twice a year the sea becomes wild and there are violent storms called equinoctial gales. They happen in March and September and last for several days. Sailors and fishermen fear them and when possible keep their ships and fishing boats safely anchored in ports until these dangerous storms are over. Some years they are more violent than others, and once in every century they are terrible.

On a Sunday morning in late September, we were dressed and ready to leave for eleven o'clock Mass in a small church in Abbeyside, near Dungarvan. As Marguerite was going to make her first communion the following spring, our little household had become markedly more religious. Wally stood at the front window, her brow wrinkled, staring up at the sky. The wind was blowing wildly and suddenly it grew very dark, a strange, evening darkness, odd so early in the morning.

"The wind is very bad," said Wally. "We won't be able to ride our bicycles—we can't go to Mass today."

She opened the front door and tried to go out. It was impossible. The wind would have knocked her down. Pushing with all her strength, she closed the door, repeating, "The weather is too bad for us to go out. We'll have to follow Mass on the wireless."

I wasn't thinking about Mass. I was standing in the porch looking at the sky, the black mountains and the bog. I didn't like what I saw. This storm was clearly different. Every sign of life had disappeared. Not a bat or a bird was to be seen, and even the ever-present seagulls had vanished. The wind was making much more noise than usual and now the distant roar of the sea was becoming louder. The tide was coming in. The enormous waves had not yet reached the shingle and as they surged closer and closer, the volume increased. What, I wondered, is going to happen next? I didn't have long to wait. Suddenly there was a terrific roar and a gigantic wave crashed over the lower part of the shingle, flooding the field behind the bungalows. Strange things began to happen. The bog was also moving and filling up with water. There was another crash, another roar, more waves. The bog was transformed into a turbulent lake, the wind making waves on its surface.

Wally and Marguerite ran from one window to another, watching the water rise around our bungalow. I remained for some time in the porch, then finally came into the living room. I had never been so frightened. The noise was deafening. I shouted to Wally, "Where is yesterday's newspaper?"

"In the kitchen," answered Wally, looking at me as if to say, have you lost your mind to want to read a newspaper in such circumstances? I found the paper and quickly opened it to the second page. I ran my finger down the bottom column to the weather report, with the all-important tide schedules. I found the listing for that day, Sunday. Wally and Marguerite were watching me in silence, their faces white with fear. In a voice that I tried to keep as matter of fact as possible, I said, "High tide is at ten fifty-five today. If we are still alive at that time, we will be saved."

We looked at our little clock—it was only ten-thirty. Each minute of the next twenty-five seemed an eternity. It was probably going to be a question of only a few minutes, I thought. We all knew from experience that the tide was never late, either coming in or going out. Time crept on. At about ten forty-five there was yet another tremendous gust of wind and the smallest bungalow on our left was suddenly uprooted from its foundations and violently blown sideways across the bog. Huge waves carried it off and it disappeared altogether.

Moments later, two other bungalows could be seen floating on their sides in the middle of the raging lake as yet another mighty wave broke over the shingle. The field behind Sunnyside was now full of water, nearly reaching the top of the protecting six-foot-high stone wall. The bog and the field in the front were filling fast with the rising water which was now infiltrating our little garden.

"We're completely surrounded now," I said.

At this point, Wally got out her rosary beads and hysterically cried, "Get on your knees. We will start saying the prayers for the dying."

"No!" I shouted, furious. "You are not dying yet—and neither am I!" I looked around the room. "The water will be in the house at any second. This is no time to be resigning ourselves and doing nothing. Let's stack up what we can as high as possible."

I couldn't pray. I kept glancing at the little clock and then at the rising water as I groped for a few clothes and put them with my precious books on top of my wardrobe. "I never killed an albatross," I said indignantly in a low voice. "Why should the sea kill me?"

Water was entering the house now. The kitchen soon flooded and in the porch we had water up to our knees. Another glance at the clock convinced me that our race with the rising water would end in a neck to neck finish, with just a nose between life and death.

"Please God, don't let us drown."

The last five minutes were truly desperate. At ten fifty, I marked with a pencil the high water marks on the wall. Marguerite stood like a statue on the living room table, hugging Biddy, her little dog. Wally stood in silence, white-faced, in the porch. We could barely move. The water was up to my waist. Finally, at eleven, I was at last convinced that the water had stopped rising. We were saved.

Wally, Marguerite and I prayed. "Maybe there is a

God after all," I thought as they, who had no doubts, prayed in shaky voices. "Our Father" followed "Hail Mary" as the storm roared and the few pieces of furniture disappeared under the water. We were all three too terrified to speak anything but our separate prayers.

When at last the water was receding faster and we could move again, Wally said, "I'll light the primus and we'll have a cup of tea." Unfortunately, the primus had drowned. Upon that sad discovery, Wally went into her bedroom and opened the top of her cupboard where she always said her private papers were kept. From there she pulled out a bottle of Jameson's whisky that I noted with astonishment was only half full. A sort of delayed hysteria was overwhelming all three of us. Wally helped herself to a large glass of whisky and downed it in two gulps. She gave us both a small amount each which, following her example, we promptly swallowed. I watched my sister give a violent shudder.

By mid-afternoon the water was not only completely out of the bungalow but also out of most of the garden. A portion of the field was becoming visible as well. I had been numbed by fright and whisky for a while, but now I was stirred into action again, by the cold.

"We must get out of here. It is far too dangerous to stay. The tide will be coming back again in a few hours, and this time high tide will be at night. We must get out!" I implored them but there was no answer from either Wally or Marguerite.

I tried to open the front door but it was jammed with mud and I didn't have enough strength. I saw there was no use calling for Wally's help—she was incapable of any sort of motion. Having taken more whisky, she refused to move. Marguerite had fallen asleep on her bed, her dog in her arms, keeping her warm. "What can I do?" I asked myself.

I was on the verge of panic, when I saw through the rain and the howling wind two men fighting their way towards us. One looked vaguely familiar. They were Coast Guards. Pushing open the front door, they entered and

Sally Scrope with Kabos-Joe.

Sunnyside and the empty lot where a cottage once stood before it was blown away in the storm.

looked around with solemn faces. The place was a terrible mess. At first no one talked and then one man ordered, "Get your things ready. We don't have any time to waste. Hurry up. We are taking you into town."

I sighed with relief. The suitcases were wet—nobody had given a thought to them. But it didn't matter—everything was wet. I put a few of my clothes and books into one suitcase. Wally seemed still unable to move so I got two more suitcases, went into Wally's room and packed them both as best I could with Wally's and Marguerite's clothes. As I worked and ran from room to room, the floor squished seawater under my naked feet.

The two men wore tall rubber boots. One picked up Marguerite in his arms, wrapping a large blanket around her. He also took a suitcase. The other man, followed by Biddy, carried the remaining two suitcases.

In the confusion, Wally could not find the key of the bungalow, so it was left unlocked. Wally and I, also wrapped in blankets and struggling against the gale-like wind, followed the two men to their car which they had left in front of Johnny and Johanna's cottage. It seemed unharmed, sitting as it did on much higher ground than ours, which was not far above sea level. I saw their white and worried faces staring at us through the window. They were alive, thank God.

As we drove into Dungarvan, the guards became more talkative. They had been watching the bungalow from the Dungarvan Road, quite unable to approach to rescue us until the tide had turned. It was "a miracle" they said, that we had not been drowned. I could well imagine what the storm had looked like as seen from the Dungarvan Road, with the flooded bog, waves breaking over the shingle, the bungalows like islands in a sea of water with three of them lying on their sides like floundered vessels. My hands and fingers were quite blue and I shivered under my blanket as the car moved closer to town. Our escape had been narrow indeed.

The senior Coast Guard was very cross with Wally. He did not mince his words telling what he thought of her.

"You must be out of your mind, woman, to think of staying out there during the time of these gales. Do what else you like, but I'll not risk my neck for you again, and I forbid you to return to Clonea Strand until April. It is much too dangerous in winter and you should have known it— you stupid woman—being no stranger to this part of the country."

I could hardly believe my ears, Wally was getting a scolding.

At last the car stopped in front of the Devonshire Arms Hotel. The two men carried both Marguerite and me into the hall. Miss Dunne, the owner of the hotel, greeted us with an anxious smile. I turned to the two men and said: "Thank you very much for saving our lives." Marguerite added a whispered, "Thank you."

Miss Dunne led us upstairs to two bedrooms, then took Marguerite and me into the bathroom and helped us take a hot bath. It was our first bath in nearly three years. Then, lending us each dry, warm clothes, she put us to bed, with a large glass of hot milk and honey.

Wally had retired directly to her room. She was too tired to bother about us and in any case she knew that we were in good hands. Having, I imagined, swallowed another glass of whisky, she had fallen asleep, so we were left to the kindness of Miss Dunne. She brought us hot water bottles and cups of hot soup. I drank mine gratefully. It tasted delicious and spread warmth through my body. My sister did not look well, quite white with a pinched little face. She tried her best but could not swallow her soup. Miss Dunne did not insist. "You will feel better in the morning. Goodnight now, sleep well and God bless you." She turned off the light and softly closed the door.

I went to sleep. It did not seem long before I was awake again. "Where am I? What is happening?" I was shivering again. Then I realized where I was and that the sound that I was hearing was my sister's voice. I switched on the electric light and went over to the other bed. Marguerite was now red, she was sweating, her speech was not normal and she was weakly calling, "Mummy . . . Mummy . . ."

"So this is delirium," I thought. I had read about it in books. No time should be lost. I opened the door, ran down the cold corridor to Wally's room and banged on the door. It was locked and I heard the familiar sound of snoring. Help would have to be found somewhere else. There was light coming from under another door, on which I knocked loudly and with desperation. To my relief, it was opened by Miss Dunne.

"Please, please, Miss Dunne. Please get the doctor. My little sister is very ill." Miss Dunne put on a green dressing gown, went into our room and gave Marguerite a quick look. Immediately she ran downstairs and I heard her speaking on the telephone.

"Tell him to come at once," I heard her say.

Soon Doctor McCarthy arrived. After a brief examination of us both, he gave us some medicine. As he spoke with Miss Dunne the words "shock" and "pneumonia" were repeated.

"Please, Doctor, my little sister must not die."

"You'll both be all right in a few days. I'll come back in the morning," he said kindly. After they had left us, I climbed into my sister's bed to keep her warm.

We stayed in bed for a week and fortunately did not develop pneumonia, only bad colds. Later on, however, we both were haunted by nightmares which occurred regularly for months and even years. My nightmare is always the same. I am naked, and to the roar of the thunder I am riding the crest of a wave—riding—swimming—sinking. Sylvia is dead and my name is Ophelia. My hair is heavy with salt, my spirit is with the water babies and my body lies at the bottom of the sea.

This was the only time during our stay in Ireland that we saw a doctor.

L IFE IN DUNGARVAN came as a welcome change after the solitude of Clonea Strand. Miss Dunne's hotel was as usual nearly empty during the winter months, and she was happy to give Wally "special financial conditions." We remained in the two bedrooms and were allowed to use a large formal sitting room, when it was not required by other clients. This room smelled of fresh polish, and was filled with heavy Victorian furniture. The chairs had white lace covers and lace curtains framed the windows overlooking the main street. Marguerite and I often sat by one of these windows, fascinated by the comings and goings of people on foot or on bicycle. It was rare to see a car.

Some evenings, before going to bed, I would sit on the top step of the staircase. From this perch I could see into the bar, watch the men drink, and listen to sad Irish songs about battles lost or loved ones who lived across the sea. There were also political discussions, during which voices often became louder. When these exchanges of opinion degenerated into a fight, which was rare, I would quickly nip back into my bedroom and lock the door.

We had our meals in the dining room with other clients, mostly men, who at midday were sometimes noisy and numerous. The food was plentiful but badly prepared. Irish cooking seemed to me a great contradiction. How could the Irish, who have so much imagination in other realms, be so totally devoid of it in a thing as essential as preparing food?

Despite being by the sea, the only fish ever served in Ireland, it seemed, were kippers. This might have been because the sea mines made captains reluctant to sail far from shore, or perhaps it was forbidden. Shrimp, mussels and oysters certainly existed along the coast, as they did in Brittany, but were never eaten by the Irish. Meat, which was rationed, was always boiled or stewed. Potatoes were the only truly plentiful foodstuff. Cabbage, parsnips and turnips were regularly served boiled. We drank water and strong black tea. The service was very slow but at least we had no peeling of vegetables or washing-up to do, and this meant more time for reading.

I could now walk every day to the technical school. Marguerite continued her rather vague lessons with Wally. We were each allowed one piano lesson a week with little Miss Delaney, a tiny woman of elfish charm, who quickly turned my do, re, mi, fa into the less classical C, D, E, F.

Slowly, I began to meet the people of Dungarvan. I found them generous and kind but it was difficult for me to make friends. I was very shy and didn't have much I wanted to say about myself. It was difficult to talk about my family and background and it only made me homesick.

I didn't dare go into their houses because this was strictly forbidden by Wally. I didn't resent this particular rule, because some Irish adults that I had met in Clonea Strand and in Dungarvan made me uncomfortable with their views about the war. They liked talking politics and were very opinionated on the subject. Certain Irish Catholics seemed to me to be crazily pro-German. Apparently they were egged on by some of the priests. I had sat in silent horror myself through several such sermons, now that we went regularly to Mass in Dungarvan and Abbeyside. They hated both the English and the Protestants to a degree that eclipsed all other considerations. None of them had ever met a German, but this didn't matter. What they seemed to enjoy above all was their former enemy, England, fighting for her very survival. Many Irish hoped that Hitler would win the war and said so. They would try to persuade me that the Germans were "a fine people" and Hitler was a "great man" and that the French nation would one day side with the Germans in an all-out effort to beat the English. Several times in church we were asked to pray for Hitler. To all this talk, I would solemnly shake my head.

"No. Never, never," I would say. I remembered what had been said about the Nazis and how they had killed so many people and persecuted the Jews. Also, my father had talked to me about the 1914–18 war. My grandfather had been wounded twice and two of his brothers had been killed at Verdun. I was certain that the French would never join Germany against Great Britain. I sometimes had the feeling that some Irish had very narrow minds, blaming England for all their woes and having no broader view of Europe as a whole. In 1943 the Irish Republic was enjoying, along with Switzerland, a peace and lack of misery unknown to the other countries of Europe. Yet, some Irish still indulged in lamenting about the past. If only, I thought to myself, they looked at themselves from time to time and gave themselves a kick in the ass. In some ways the war had made me tough and I could not bring myself to feel sorry for these men singing sad songs of years ago and feeling oh so sorry for themselves as they drank too much in the warm comfort of the Devonshire Arms. If they had been unlucky in the past, they were damned lucky at the moment.

"The Germans are great people, to be sure," they would repeat doggedly, nodding their heads.

No one paid attention to a young girl who spoke with a Dungarvan brogue and who would sometimes hear hushed voices talk about German submarines hiding and refueling in small Irish ports, not far east of where we stood. It was no secret and although I never actually saw a German submarine, there seemed to be no doubt about it. At the same time, Ireland being Ireland, other Irish men and women were bravely fighting the Germans in the RAF, the Royal Navy and the Army. Some were killed, a lot were wounded and many were heroes.

IT WAS WHILE STAYING IN THE HOTEL in Dungarvan that at last Marguerite found a friend. A bright little girl with sparkling eyes, red hair, a turned up nose and freckles, her name was Maura. Like my sister, she was also learning how to play the piano. After school, Maura often came to the hotel and then, with Wally's permission, the two children would go for long walks, exchanging secrets as all little girls do. I was very pleased that she had at last found a friend. She looked much happier. She would talk and smile, sometimes even laugh. Biddy, the white Maltese terrier, would accompany them everywhere. They became a common sight on the safe streets of Dungarvan, not bothered by so much as a car. They were a happy trio and it made my heart glad to see them.

Now that I no longer had the ten-mile bicycle ride and shopping to do, I was free after school to explore the countryside around the little town. That is how, one day in early spring, I passed by a large house surrounded by a low wall and a well-kept garden. It practically burst with hundreds of varieties of daffodils, all in bloom. It was a beautiful scene and quite different from the scrappy yards of most of the houses. I stopped, put one foot on the low wall and, still sitting on my old black bicycle, sat quietly admiring the flowers.

"How do you do?" said a small woman who had been weeding behind a shrub and whom I had not spotted.

"Oh, I'm very well, thank you," I answered, looking at the thin elderly lady.

"Do you like my garden?"

"Yes, I love it. I have never before seen so many different kinds of daffodils. I did not know that there were so many. Do you do all the work yourself?" I asked with admiration.

"Nearly all," said the kind lady. "Who are you? I know most of the Dungarvan children, I've never seen you before."

"That's not surprising," I answered, her well-educated accent giving me confidence, "because, you see, I don't belong to Dungarvan. I'm French and have been living out on Clonea Strand with my little sister and my governess. We're now staying at the Devonshire Arms because our bungalow was flooded during the big storm. We were nearly drowned," I added. Now that the adventure was over, a certain amount of interest could be derived from mentioning our frightening experience and narrow escape.

"Oh! so you are one of the French girls. I have heard about you. Do come into the rectory and meet my husband. It is tea time and I have made some fresh scones."

Forgetting Wally's rule, I was delighted to accept the lady's invitation. She was friendly, and the garden was truly beautiful. As we walked slowly toward the house, she talked to me kindly about her flowers.

"September and early October are the best months for planting daffodil bulbs. In good weather, during these two months, I plant some every week. I have made a study of these flowers, for they are the ones I love best of all. There are hundreds of different varieties. These, for instance, are Cyclamineus. They are a species of dwarf daffodils. Growing beside them is a stand of salmon-crowned Blarney. By the oak tree you have a group of pure white Cantatrice and over there, by the fence, some lemon-tinted Hunter's Moon. By the gate are the robust Golden Harvest that make such beautiful long-lasting bouquets for the house. Outside a cottage or a castle, there is always a place for daffodils," she said firmly, as she opened the door of the rectory. The hall led into a room that was obviously a library. I felt it was a happy home.

"This is my husband, the Reverend Desmond Lang," the lady said. "He is a parson."

"My name is Sylvia Couturié. I am French," I said, introducing myself.

To my immense surprise, the Reverend Lang repeated my name with the correct pronunciation. As he rose to greet me, I saw that he was very tall. With his delicate features and deep-set eyes, it seemed to me that this man was of a different race than the other men of Dungarvan.

"He must be a scholar," I thought. I liked them both enormously.

Mrs. Lang disappeared into the kitchen and I was able to examine the room. Except for the door and windows, it was entirely lined with books. These books, many with colored leather bindings and gold lettering, were very different from those in the lending library. My host told me that he had read them all, loved them all and was very proud of them. They were both his friends and his treasure.

Soon his wife returned with the tea tray which she placed on a low table. She set alight the kindling in the fireplace and the good dry wood soon crackled cheerfully. As I ate the hot scones spread with delicious homemade strawberry jam, I relaxed and smiled, grateful to be soaking up the warmth of this happy home.

"What is your favorite pastime?" asked the parson.

"Reading and playing tennis," came the prompt reply.

"And what books have you read?"

"I've read nearly all the books in the Dungarvan library," I said with confidence. "I started with Charles Dickens. *Oliver Twist* was the first book I ever read in English, and then I read all his other books that I could find." I continued, giving the names of the other authors whose books I had read: Sir Walter Scott, Jane Austen, the Brontë sisters, Swift, Tolstoy, Thackeray, Milton, Chaucer, Kipling and a little Shakespeare.

"There are a lot of other books I would very much like to read, but unfortunately they are banned by the Irish Catholic censorship, works of genius notwithstanding. I've seen their names, but I'll have to wait: Bernard Shaw, Graham Greene, William Faulkner, Ernest Hemingway, Aldous Huxley, Anatole France, James Joyce and so many others that can't be found in Ireland. I've also read and learned a lot of poetry, but you cannot imagine all the problems I have . . ."

My hosts were wonderful listeners. They had not interrupted me, and words came pouring out.

"What are your problems?" asked the holy man.

"I have two major problems. The first one is that I only have a small dictionary, and often there are words I don't understand which aren't listed. So I try to guess their meaning, but sometimes it doesn't make sense."

"I can help you with that," said the reverend. "Write a list of the words you don't understand and I will explain them to you. Had you studied Latin and Greek, of course, you would not have this difficulty."

"I would love to study Latin and Greek," I said wistfully. "I did start Latin in France when I was ten, but I've forgotten it all."

"And what is your other problem?"

"My other problem is quite different, but a nuisance all the same. As I've just told you, I've read quite a lot of books, but in a haphazard way. I know nothing about the men and women who wrote them. When did they live? In what country? When did they die? For all I know, they could all have lived more or less at the same time, in the same place, and that just couldn't be. It's most confusing. You see, I didn't go to school for three years, and in Clonea Strand we didn't have any schoolbooks for either history or geography. I'm hopeless in arithmetic. I can remember some French history but I have never learned any other. Of course I've read in other books about Oliver Cromwell, the Irish famine and the "troubles" and I felt very sorry for the poor Irish, especially the women and children, but I have never clearly understood why all this came about.

"Don't worry. I understand your problems and they can be solved. I'll lend you a book that you must study carefully. You can bring it back next week. Then, if you have other questions, I'll try to answer them. But it will be hard work."

"I don't mind hard work," I said with a smile.

He stood up, went directly to a shelf beside his desk and selected a book. "Here is a volume that will help you: *The History of English Literature in the 17th, 18th and 19th Centuries.*"

"Thank you very much," I said as he handed it to me.

Mrs. Lang had remained silent, but now she asked, "You said that you liked tennis? I'm too old for that game nowadays, but I like to play golf. Next week, when you bring back the book, we can go to the golf course and I will be happy to show you how to play. It is very different from tennis but it's a fine game. Afterwards we can come back here for tea and talk about books."

"Oh, thank you—thank you very much," I said, looking at the clock. Oh, horrors, it was later than I thought. I hastily picked up the book and shook hands solemnly with my new friends.

"Goodbye, goodbye. I will come back next week." I said.

The bicycle ride back to the hotel was accomplished in minutes. I could scarcely believe my good fortune. I was so delighted with my new friends who had been kind and sympathetic. I was bubbling over with the news and stupidly rushed in to tell it to Wally and Marguerite, proudly showing them the beautiful book. Due to my exhilaration and excitement, I was not immediately aware of Wally's changing mood. Gradually, her stony silence drew my gaze to her face. It had darkened, the muscles had become tense, her eyes seemed even smaller than usual, her mouth a thin line. She didn't shout or hit me, for fear that someone in the hotel might hear her. She picked up the book and, without even looking at the title, carried it into her room. Seconds later she was back. She stood very close, though she didn't touch me. In a low voice, she hissed like a snake, "You ass, you idiot. How dare you forget that you are a Catholic. Mr. Lang and his wife are Protestants and, what makes things even worse, he is a parson. How can you be such a fool? You are certainly never going to read any books coming from that place. The Langs would be only too pleased to brag about it. They would try to make you abandon your faith. By lending you a book, by giving you scones and tea, they are trying to lure you away from your church. This nonsense I must stop at once and there must be no scandal. Sylvia, you will go back to the rectory next week and return the book. You will politely refuse any others, then go to the golf course with Mrs. Lang. Afterwards, never, and I mean never, cross their doorstep or speak to them again. I will keep an eye on you so that you don't!"

The utter stupidity of the situation made me sad rather than angry. I had learned nothing, it seemed. I should have known better and not told Wally. In an effort to hide my sadness, I went back to a series of shorthand exercises, saying under my breath "Damn—damn—damn—damn!"

At the end of the following week, Wally gave me back *The History of English Literature* and I cycled to the rectory. The daffodils were in even fuller bloom, a crown of color around the house. Mrs. Lang opened the door. "Ah! There you are. Come in," she said cheerfully, taking the book from my hands and putting it on the oak table in the hall. "It's a nice day. My husband is occupied in his study for the next hour or so. Would you like to come with me to the golf course?"

"Yes, I'd love to."

When we reached the windy golf course that bordered the seafront, Mrs. Lang showed me how to place the small ball on a tee and how to hold the golf club. Then she proceeded to hit several balls one after the other with a graceful swing that sent the ball sharply into the air over a long distance. It was then my turn. The club felt long and heavy and proved difficult to control. With an energetic swing, I hit the ground and the ball remained immobile. At last I did manage to hit the ball but it did not go very far and the next ones were not much better. I was not really in the mood for games.

"Don't worry," said my kind instructor. "It's not an easy game to learn and it takes a lot of practice. You'll do better next week."

On our return, Mrs. Lang remarked, "You are very quiet today. What's the matter, dear? Have you had bad news from France?"

"No, we have not heard from our parents for several months now. That's not why I'm upset."

Wisely she did not pursue the matter. We walked into the house, entering the friendly book-filled room where her husband, reading by a cheerful fire, was waiting for us.

It was no fault of theirs that the pleasant atmosphere of the previous week had evaporated completely. It was my fault. I was nervous, embarrassed and very sad.

"Did you find what you were looking for in the book I lent you?" inquired my host.

"I did not even open it," I answered in a low voice. "Wally, my governess, would not allow me to. She confiscated it. She said that I was not to read any book coming from the rectory." I nearly added "because you are Protestants" but that would have been too rude to say to these kind people. Instead I said, "I am Catholic, you see. Also, Wally has forbidden me to come back here or play golf with Mrs. Lang. And she also said that she would make sure I didn't disobey her. I am terribly, terribly sorry. There is nothing I can do. Please understand. I cannot be either disobedient or disloyal to her," I added lamely.

The Reverend Desmond Lang was a quiet man with an even temper. He had self-discipline and a certain philosophy of life to which was added a deeply rooted desire to try to understand the problems of other people. He had chosen to be a minister of the church and, as in the gospel, he wanted to be a fatherly shepherd. And yet, by nature, he had a violent temper that he managed to control. When I had finished talking, however, his face was red and flushed. It was obvious that he was having great difficulty suppressing his natural feelings. He did not speak. What was there to say? Situations like these arose and still arise in Ireland to this very day. A country of Christians at daggers drawn, Catholics and Protestants politely drinking tea together and yet never allowed by their clergy to become friends. I always found it very odd that both sides staunchly maintained that they were Christians. I suppose neither side ever thought what Christ might have felt about their strange behavior, so foreign to his teachings. This was Ireland, Holy Ireland, land of saints and nonsense.

As soon as I had finished tea, I stood up to say goodbye. As I shook hands with the parson, I looked intently at his face and knew I would never forget him. After a lingering look at the lovely books lining the walls of the room, I followed Mrs. Lang to the door. I extended my hand and sadly said goodbye. She held my hand and then surprised me with a soft kiss on my cheek. This unexpected act of tenderness was too much for me, and I burst into tears.

"Don't cry," said Mrs. Lang.

"No. I'll be all right," I answered, climbing on to my bike with tears streaming down my face.

I could not tell her that the reason I was crying was because no one, absolutely no one, had softly kissed my cheek for more than three years.

"*Merde!*" I said to myself. "I thought I would never cry again and here I am behaving like a baby. And what is worse, I have now broken my promise to Mr. Churchill."

TONY LAWN WAS MY FIRST BOYFRIEND. A student at the Dungarvan Technical School, arithmetic was his favorite subject. This influenced him and he wanted to become an accountant. Tony, at fifteen and a half, was tall for his age. He had a pleasant face, topped by a mop of brown curly hair that, like most boys of his age, he was often combing. He was quite pleased with his looks now that his face was clear of pimples. His parents owned a cloth shop near the post office in the Dungarvan main square. The outside of the shop was painted black and over the only door, in gold letters, the name Lawn was written. The Lawns sold a variety of materials for men's suits. Both windows of the small shop were filled with bolts of cloth of different shades and quality; fine cloth for Sundays and feast days and bolts of thick tweed for everyday wear.

After school, Tony and I would walk back to the square together. There were hardly ever any cars. He had good manners, always walking on the outer side of the footpath and carrying my schoolbooks along with his own.

On reaching the square, we would go our separate ways, making the sign of the cross before crossing each street, in the improbable case of a mortal car accident. This was supposed to get us straight to heaven. I thought the much greater risk was to be caught by Wally and have her give me hell.

One winter afternoon, Miss Patterson, our English teacher, did not appear. She had the flu and Dr. McCarthy had told her to stay in bed. The boys and girls of her class were free either to stay in the classroom to study or go home. I saw no point of going back so early to the hotel. School was far more pleasant. Slowly, the other boys and girls left until finally I was alone with Tony.

"You really are bad at arithmetic. If you don't improve, you'll never pass the accounting examination. Would you like me to help you with tomorrow's lesson?" suggested Tony.

"Yes, please, that's a great idea."

"You'll have trouble with tomorrow's work. I'll find something simpler first." He selected an easy problem and with great patience explained how it should be solved. Alas, I could not work it out by myself, even after his careful explanation.

Finally, Tony sighed and said, "It's hopeless. You'll never be any good at accounting. You aren't stupid, but not gifted. You don't really care, that is what I really think!"

"Of course I care because I want to learn, but also in another way you are right, I don't," I laughed. "I know that I should try harder and perhaps I would if only you had the metric system. It's so much easier. You have such beautiful silver coins in Ireland. It's lovely shopping to pay for things like boring groceries with salmon, greyhounds and horses engraved on pretty silver coins."

"Be serious, can't you?" said Tony, rather crossly.

"I am very serious," I said solemnly, and explained my idea. "If you had, for instance, ten salmon for one greyhound and ten greyhounds for one horse, your way of counting would be much more logical."

Tony shook his head. "No, that is perhaps a pity but it is quite impossible."

I did not see why and remained silent.

Changing the subject, he asked, "What would you do if you were rich one day?"

"I really don't know. I don't need much money. I love boiled eggs, baked potatoes and green apples and they are never expensive anywhere. I only need money for books."

"And what about Woodbines?" asked Tony.

"To be sure, I need a little money for Woodbines. A girl can have a few faults . . ." I had started to smoke in secret and this was the cheapest brand available.

"Well, I'll tell you something. I don't think that you'll ever be rich because you'll never know how to count."

"Of course I'll never be rich. Money is made to be earned and spent. It isn't meant, as you seem to think, to be stored in a bank. Yes, Tony Lawn, to be sure you're right, I'll never be rich because I don't care as much as most people do about money and I don't suppose that I ever will. I was born with a silver spoon in my mouth, as people say, and then because of the war became poor. Ever since I was twelve, I've made and mended my clothes and most of my sister's. For years we lived in a little wooden cottage, with neither heating, running water, electricity nor even a proper lavatory, and with no family of any kind. No parents, no grandmothers, no dear aunts and uncles, or cousins for fun and games. I also know that, if I don't love money for money's sake, I do love beautiful things and think that a thing of beauty is a joy forever. I am sentimental about objects that I have known and loved even if they have no financial value. They must have warmth and beauty. Having a lot of money isn't essential."

I put my hand in my pocket and pulled out a few coins, two salmon, three greyhounds and a horse. I showed them to my friend. "This is my whole fortune," I whispered with a smile.

"You also have something else," said Tony looking at me seriously.

"Now what would that be, if you please?"

"A pretty face."

"Oh, shut up!" I smiled happily.

"Come on, Mavourneen, time is passing and if you are late, Wally might break your lovely neck."

"To be sure she would break it if she knew that I was alone in the classroom with you. I had better look out because I only have the one," I laughed. We left the school together in the pouring rain.

Unfortunately, Wally did hear about Tony Lawn and that he was carrying my books home from school each day.

"You'll end up in the gutter," she shouted one evening when she knew that Miss Dunne was out. "I have always said so. You won't go far and you will end up in the gutter."

"I don't think so at all," I answered, "I've always loved to wash."

"That is not what I mean, you brat," she yelled, then sat down to write a letter to her sister Madge, puffing away at a cigarette for the good of her sensitive nerves.

When I had finished my homework, I went to my room, got my book and curled up in a large armchair in the living room. Not wanting Wally to know how much I was reading, and afraid of her disapproval of authors whom she did not know, I wrapped my book in the very safe cover of *David Copperfield*. I knew from experience that Charles Dickens was safe from Wally. What I was really reading was Milton's *Paradise Lost*. I found it fascinating, although not always easy to understand. I often had recourse to the dictionary and it was slow going with no teacher to explain.

Wally, sitting across from me, eventually said crossly, "Why are you reading again instead of knitting or sewing? Do you have no more stockings to mend? You are a lazy girl and you are also the slowest reader I know."

"Yes, I mean no. The stockings are all mended," I answered. I did not move nor raise my eyes because I knew that my eyes were filled with hate. Silently I added, "I am not lazy, I am just learning, you silly old witch. Reading is my only escape, my path to freedom."

*F*OR CHRISTMAS 1943, with the money my grandmother had sent me from America, I bought a little harmonica and, in bed at night, I played softly for my sister and myself. I learned to play lovely Irish songs and ballads quite easily by myself, and it was not difficult to pick out a tune. I always kept my harmonica either in my pocket or safely hidden under the mattress, along with a pack of Woodbines, my books from the library and the torch which enabled me to read at night.

Aunt Sylvia, whom we had never met, regularly wrote charming affectionate letters telling us about our little American cousins. She sent photos of her children. These helped us to visualize our unknown relatives.

We received no letters from France or Switzerland, but to our surprise, a few days before Christmas a letter arrived with a Berlin postmark. It was from Alexander Albert, a German officer who had married an American cousin of my mother's.

We had no idea before receiving this letter that we had a German relative. We went on reading and learned that Alexander Albert had been in France, had seen our mother and wanted us to know that both our parents were well. It was a kind and affectionate letter. He had not seen his wife or children for several years, he said, and he could understand how lonely we must be. His letter ended by sending us his fondest love and was signed "Uncle Alex."

"To be sure, he must be a very nice man, our Uncle Alex. I wonder what he looks like," said Marguerite.

"He cannot be really nice; don't forget, he's a German and all Germans are horrid," I answered, thinking of the air raids.

Finally we both decided that Uncle Alex was an exception. I wrote to him at his Berlin address, but as no other letter arrived, we never knew if he received my carefully written lines. That was the sad fate of a very large amount of wartime correspondence. Meantime the war continued, more fiercely than ever. Grown-up people fought while children listened and watched, waited and died.

We had very few photographs with us. We had one of our mother and one of our father standing with a walking stick and his cocker spaniel in front of the house. We also had a picture postcard of the back of the château in which we were born. Time makes everyone forget. Some nights, in bed, I would close my eyes and concentrate very hard. No, there was nothing I could do about it. I had forgotten what my father and mother looked like. I knew that my sister also tried, with even less success. Photographs help, I thought, but they do not replace the distant or the dead.

Christmas always made me feel particularly homesick. It had always been such a family feast. It was certainly not because of the excitement of presents because at Le Mesnil we were always given a toy each on the 6th of December, the feast of Saint Nicolas. On the same day a small crèche was placed on the mantelpiece in our nursery with porcelain figures of the Virgin Mary, Saint Joseph, an ox, a donkey and a few sheep. During Christmas night someone would place the child Jesus in his manger and on Christmas day we would gaze at him in wonder. We would also find at the bottom of our bed a stocking full of small toys. In our village church there was also a very beautiful medieval crèche surrounded by a multitude of burning candles. My favorite hymn was "Silent Night." At Le Mesnil on Christmas day we were allowed to have lunch with our parents, a special privilege. We always had an immense roast turkey, a present sent every year to my parents by Lord Derby. One year my father even sent me to the kitchen, insisting that I be weighed with the turkey. He was greatly amused because he had rightly guessed that the turkey was heavier than I, although I was already eight years old.

There was also always a brightly flaming Christmas

pudding with a twig of holly placed on top, an annual present from Mrs. Diggle who lived in Yorkshire. The first Christmas tree I ever saw was in 1938. It was in the drawing-room of my American grandmother's flat in Paris. Christmas trees and all that went with them were not part of French tradition and as a child I never saw one at Le Mesnil.

Clonea Strand with the Ocean View Hotel in the distance, the beach with its rocks, and the little wooden bungalows to the right, with the bog just beyond them.

CHAPTER SEVEN

The Secret

O N THE FIRST DAY OF APRIL 1944, we left the Devon-shire Arms Hotel and returned to our much less expensive "Sunnyside" at Clonea Strand.

A few weeks later we received a letter from Lady Waterford saying that she would send her car for us the following week so that we could spend a day at Curraghmore. Over the years she had done her best, without success, to persuade Wally that we all live with her at Curraghmore and be sent at her expense to a proper school. She did not think that Dungarvan "Tech" was appropriate for me, although it was better than nothing. She was silent about the fact that Marguerite had not gone to school at all since the Waterford convent when she was nine years old. But Wally had been adamant and as a result Marguerite, now thirteen years old, was effectively illiterate. She could barely read or write in English and had forgotten every word of French. Unlike me she was never fascinated by books, although I often urged her to read mine, and I was troubled by her education, or lack of it.

On a pleasant day in early May, the chauffeur drove the ancient car with its precious rationed petrol over the narrow bumpy Dungarvan road to Waterford and up the rhododendron-lined avenue to our friend's home. There we had lunch in the main dining room for the first time. I was fascinated because it was the loveliest room I had ever seen.

I admired the delicate blue and white plasterwork on the ceiling and walls. I wondered by whom and when it had been so beautifully decorated.

There were ten people sitting around the large table: Lady Waterford and her unmarried sister Winnie Lindsay, who had always lived with her, Colonel Silcock, who was on leave, old Lady Susan Dawnay, the boys' aunt who had come over from Whitfield Court, Tyrone and Patrick, their nanny, Wally and Marguerite and me.

Only the grown-ups talked, and never about the war, during meals. We younger people answered when spoken to. The heavy silver knives and forks, the kind I had not seen for several years, reminded me of home, as did some of the portraits that looked down on us from the walls.

After lunch we all went back as a group to the drawing room. There, after a little while, Lady Susan Dawnay, my friend Blanche's grandmother, said to me, "Come with me into the garden. I want to talk to you." She was silent as we walked across the forecourt and into the rose garden. Apparently the secrets of several generations of this family were confided in this safe and lovely spot. "You must promise not to repeat to anyone what I am going to tell you," she said after making certain that we were alone. "I promise," I answered. I was now too old, I thought, to cross my throat, but I did so mentally and listened in fascinated silence. Soon I realized that she was giving me information of the highest and most secret importance. Little did I know that I would be one of the extremely rare people to share the most guarded secret of the Second World War, a secret that was not even confided to General de Gaulle.

Lady Susan knew how worried I was about my parents and my country. I was deeply grateful to her for the faith she had in me; she knew that I would not talk. She cleared her throat and said in a low voice, "Someone I know very well has been home on leave and he has told me that if the weather is good the Allies will land in Normandy on the 6th of June. That will be the perfect night, with no moon. The

Allies can only land if the weather is calm and if there is not much wind. The tide, which is most important, will also be coming in at the right time. There will be a terrible battle. If they can't land on the 6th because of the weather, the invasion will have to be postponed for several weeks. You must not worry if you don't hear from your parents for a long time. If things go as planned they won't be in the main battle area. Once we have landed in Normandy you will receive no more news from them until their part of France is liberated, and that will take several weeks or maybe several months."

"I understand," I said. "Thank you for telling me. It's a great relief to know, and you can be certain that I won't tell anyone. Please tell me what I can do to help?"

She was quiet for a moment and then said with a new weariness in her voice, "You are still a very young girl and I am an old woman. My sons and nephews will be in the battle. All we can do is hope and pray."

"I would prefer to pray in your church. It is a kinder one than mine."

"You do not have to pray in a church, Sylvia dear. The best place is under the open sky."

"I won't forget," I promised.

Then the stately old gray-haired lady and the young girl walked silently back to the house, each brave in her own way, where the whole family had tea together.

In the car on the slow drive back to Clonea Strand, I did not say a single word. In bed that night I counted. There were twenty-seven days left until what was to be D Day. As I had once done in boarding school, looking forward to home and holidays, I started to cross off each passing day on my calendar.

Bicycling to school, anxiously watching the weather, I did not often sing or whistle as had been my habit. Something long dormant in me had been awakened by Lady Dawnay's confidence. I felt a part of something larger. Bonds that had frayed—to family and country—now reasserted themselves. A sober, serious hope took hold of my heart. Great events loomed. And in their coming to pass, my own hopes might be fulfilled.

Once in school I kept away from my friends, even from Mai. My excuse was that I was working hard for my exams, which was true. Miss Patterson had devised a new method to increase the speed of our typing, as the finals approached. She would put on a record and we would type to the rhythm of military marches.

My secret knowledge somehow opened a gulf between me and the others. It was as though I was a part of things they did not understand, part of a secret society that was steeling itself to take back the world and put it right.

The good weather held up and when it did rain it was soft Irish rain with little or no wind. When the sun shone on Sunday afternoons, I would take a book and go to my haven among the high rocks at the end of the beach. There I would read and stare out to sea. One Sunday, I heard voices. People were walking in the field along the ridge of the high cliff just above where I was quietly sitting. The gentle wind carried their words to me. A man's voice said, "That's the French girl." I didn't move—silence. "Wonder what she looks like," said a woman. "I'll show you," said the man and a stone fell a few yards from where I sat. I glanced up and saw five people, two men and three women. Two more small stones fell, this time much closer. I felt trapped. Luckily, I knew the high and slippery rocks, so holding my book in my hand, barefooted I climbed swiftly over them towards the safety of the breaking waves. As I sat down again, breathing faster, I felt a strange sensation, as though a tiny crack had opened in my heart.

AS THE DAYS PASSED, I watched the weather even more closely and would panic at the sight of every cloud. On the whole, it remained beautiful, a lovely month of May. At last June arrived and there were only a few more days to wait.

"Please God, keep the weather fine." On the evening of the 5th of June I was unable to swallow my supper. Luckily, Wally failed to notice. We listened to the news on the BBC and there was nothing special. Afterwards came the French broadcast from London, *"Les Français parlent aux Français"*—the French speak to the French—and there too all was normal, nothing to awaken suspicion. The same number of messages, and as usual some that had never been heard before. And yet, Radio Londres was telling the men and women of the Resistance that the greatest moment of the war was imminent. One message was *"A l'ombre blanche des pommiers en fleurs . . ."* "I repeat," said the voice from London, "In the white shadow of apple trees in bloom . . ."

Wally decided that it was time for prayers and for bed. Later, safely in my room, I did not take off my dress or my long woolen sweater. I opened wide my window and sat on the side of my bed. I could neither read nor sleep, and like so many that night I waited.

It was a moonless night, the clouds were low and there was a strong breeze. At last, well after midnight, I climbed out of my window and over the low wall that surrounded the bungalow. I turned to the left, not going near the bog, my thoughts this night far from fairies in green dresses and the Children of the Mist. I kept close to the row of four empty bungalows until I reached the shingles. Climbing over these I stood at last on the soft sand of the wide dark beach. The tide was low and the sea far out, but I could hear the waves and walked towards them until I felt the water on my feet. Then I stood and listened. "God," I said aloud, the icy water lapping my feet, remembering my promise to Lady Dawnay, "Lord God, please save as many as you can." Moving away from the waves I knelt on the wet sand beside a heap of black seaweed and there I prayed as I had never prayed before. I hoped that He would hear the voice of a small creature with hair falling over her face and her heart trembling in her throat. In the stillness of the night, not moving, I listened, and after a while I thought that far, far away I could hear, very faintly, across the waves, the noise of bombing, the noise of war. The Allies were shelling, the invasion had begun. Men were dying on another beach. I thought that I could smell the warm blood, see in horror the brains, the lungs and the limbs, a terrible feast for the crabs, at dawn, on the beaches of Normandy. I thought that I could hear more noise than ever before covering the awful screams for help, of pain and terror, the land mines and the sea mines exploding, the silent drowning and ever more men pushing each other forward, up the beaches of Normandy toward death in the name of freedom, and others toward life and freedom. If there is a God, He must be with these heroic men tonight and I prayed until suddenly I saw that night had become another day, the sixth day of June, 1944.

I walked quickly back to the bungalow, and trembling with cold went into the kitchen and lit the primus to make some hot tea. I turned on the wireless as low as possible and put my ear against it, listening to the BBC. A man's excited voice was saying "the Allies have landed on the Normandy beaches, there is fierce fighting and the Germans are retreating." I turned the dial of the radio to the loudest so that Wally and Marguerite could hear, and I rushed into their room crying, "Wake up! Wake up! The Allies have landed, and we are going to win the war." Even Wally was swept up in it. She lit a "victory" cigarette and promised to listen to the bulletins all day. I slid two potatoes into my pocket and bicycled to school, whistling all the way. The weather was grim, the clouds low and a strong offshore breeze blowing.

At the school, everyone was talking about "The Landing." When our classes were over I peddled back to Clonea Strand as fast as possible, in order to be able to get back to the BBC and the latest thrilling news. Over the next few days we learned the strange new names given to the Normandy beaches: Sword, Juno, Gold, Omaha, Utah. "Operation Overlord" had succeeded.

There were thousands of wounded and thousands of dead. On June 7, 1944, British troops marched into Bayeux. On the 12th, American forces captured Carentan. June 13 brought bad news: the first flying bombs had landed in southern Britain. On June 14, 1944, General Charles de Gaulle set foot in liberated France.

On the same day a heavy secret weight on the shoulders of a young French girl in Ireland slowly lifted. As I ran into my room with a flushed and shiny face to change into my bathing suit, I caught my reflection in the long, narrow mirror that was fixed onto the door of my little wardrobe. I could see myself full length and yet I was staring at someone that I did not recognize. Had I changed and grown so much without noticing? Or was the reflected light of the sun setting over the bog and the crimson mountains playing tricks on me? I looked at my honey-colored hair, dark blue eyes and tanned skin and thought to myself, I am pretty—what a pleasant surprise.

In late June a friend of Wally's, Father Quaid, started to come regularly to our bungalow to prepare Marguerite for her first communion. He was a heavyset man with a dark red face and a square jaw. One time he wanted me to confess my sins to him. As I neither liked nor trusted him, I flatly refused. Both he and Wally were furious, and I got a "good talking to" from both of them about the flames of hell. These "talks" neither frightened me nor made me change my mind. That evening I went as usual for my swim in the icy Irish sea.

Afterward, I returned to the bungalow and found to my relief that Father Quaid had left after tea and cake. I put on my dress and my thick pair of winter gloves and went to the hedge along the road beyond Johnny Maloney's cottage where I found a large quantity of young green nettles. Carefully I picked a large bouquet. Holding it safely in front of me I returned to the cottage and told Wally that I had read in an old book that fresh young nettles and potatoes make a good soup. "Could we try, please?" I coaxed her. As Wally liked to cook, this put her into a better mood and together we made the soup, carefully adding salt, pepper, a tiny piece of butter and a drop of milk. It turned out to be delicious and we had a happy evening. I promised I would pick more nettles the following week.

The school year drew to an end and I passed my exams with mediocre marks. I had trouble concentrating. I also passed two Irish Red Cross Society examinations, one for first aid, the other in home nursing. I had no trouble with the written components, but I nearly fainted during the orals because of my shyness. I knew the answers, but was quickly reduced to simply shaking my head either up and down or side to side. The examiner understood and was most kind.

NEAR THE END OF THE MONTH, we learned that the British VIII Corps had launched "Operation Epson," the drive on Caen, between June 26 and June 30. Reports came in of heavy fighting and of many French civilians among the casualties. There had been no news of our parents since D Day, but I was not overly worried, because so far there had been no major battles reported in the Sarthe.

By the first of July, the Clonea Strand bungalows were all open and occupied once more for the summer. For the first time I ignored Wally's orders and talked for long hours to the other children and their parents, most of them from nearby Clonmel. I found them friendly and kind. One pretty girl named Frances Kelleher I remember vividly. With very curly blond hair and blue eyes, she was always cheerful and had many pretty clothes. She was an only child, rare in Ireland, and her parents doted on her, the lucky girl. It was with her that I learned all about lipstick and rouge, mascara and face powder. We had a lovely time painting our faces, and it was the only time in those sad days that thoughts of the war receded. I was very careful to

Me with my friends who passed the Red Cross Certificate. *Left to right:* Maureen McGowan, Leish Power, myself and Josie McManus.

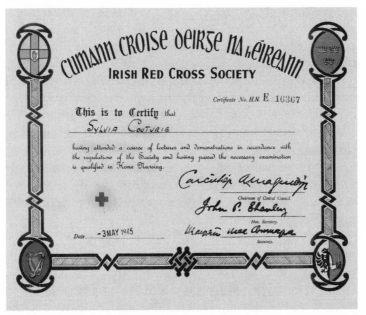

scrub my face clean before returning to Sunnyside. Even my newfound self-confidence was not enough to risk what Wally would do to me if she spotted traces of makeup.

Sometimes we smoked Woodbines, and in the evening, if the tide was low, we would go for long walks on the beach before bedtime. On Saturday nights, near the hotel, lovers would lie in each other's arms on the sand. So as not to be recognized they covered their heads and bodies with a rug, but their feet always stuck out. Frances and I didn't dare get too close, but from a distance, when the heaps moved up and down, they looked like bizarre caterpillars, a tangle of feet at one end.

Some days when the weather was fine we played tennis or picked up other people's tennis balls in front of the Ocean View Hotel. Our summer friendship ended when she returned to Clonmel with her parents at the end of August, but the effects of her friendship left me a happier person.

Time dragged on. Anxious about the war, I often couldn't sleep and I would climb out of my window and go and stand alone near the sea and look at the stars. While looking and dreaming, I sometimes heard the Irish music coming from the hotel, calling me, but I never went back. I could not bear watching people dancing while thinking of others who were dying.

I had grown up a lot, and I understood more things. I had seen photos and read the newspapers, and the lists of casualties weighed heavily on my heart. I remember hating the word itself—"casualties." How can there be anything casual about dead or wounded men, blinded, paralyzed, or losing limbs. Sometimes I had nightmares. I would hear pitched screams of terror and wake up to hear my own voice, or I would hear little children crying and wake with my own face wet with tears.

On August 25, 1944, Allied troops entered Paris. My joy was without bounds, real hope rose in my heart. By September, I knew that I would leave Ireland, hopefully soon. One warm afternoon I walked slowly for several hours in my sweet smelling bog. I lay in the grass and listened to the humming of insects and watched the butterflies. I picked my last bouquet of delicate wildflowers, and murmured farewell to all the delightful Little People of my imagination.

The Clonea Strand bungalows closed one by one, and soon Sunnyside would as well. School started, and I was happy to study again and especially to see Mai. She immediately asked me if I had any news of my parents, and I could only shake my head no. It had been three months since the Allies had landed in Normandy, and Paris had been liberated, but the Germans were still trying to hold on in France and there was heavy regional fighting.

The V1 and V2 rockets were raining down on Britain, and there were still daily reports of death and destruction on the BBC. We didn't know whether our parents were alive or dead, or whether Le Mesnil had been bombed or burnt. Consumed with my worry, and often irritable, I found it difficult to concentrate on shorthand and typing.

Reading remained the greatest escape. Miss Patterson had lent me a fascinating old book about Celtic Countries, in which I discovered the ABC equivalent is bath–luis–nuin. The Celtic alphabet is not the ABC we know. It consists of eighteen letters, each letter represented by the name of a tree—for example, Oak, Birch, Rowen, Ash, Ivy, Furze, Heather, Aspen. In Gaelic they run today as follows: Ailm, Breite, Call, Dur, Eagh, Fearn, and so on, with their strange slightly Arabic sounds. How curious and magical, I thought, that Celtic men had chosen the names of trees to learn to read. I wish I had been able to learn at least a little Irish, but now it was too late. I also borrowed Irish history books, but tended to skip much of what they contained, famines and wars being too upsetting for me. I had little need of old battles. World War II was more than enough for me.

One autumn day, with the sun shining into our classroom, we were sitting straight in our chairs, typing in rhythm to Miss Patterson's choice of the day's music. Suddenly, my brain went into a whirl. I couldn't control my mind and my fingers refused to type. I collapsed on my desk. Everyone stared at my shaking body. "Child, what on earth is the matter?" asked Miss Patterson. Then, faintly, I heard Mai's anxious, indignant voice. "The music!" she said, "It's the 'Marseillaise'—you have made her type to the notes of her national anthem . . !" "Sorry," said Miss Patterson, and she put on another record. After a while I calmed down and was able to resume typing. Later Mai told me that everyone was very upset at having seen me in "such a state," especially poor Miss Patterson.

At long last, at the end of October, four months after the Allies landed in France, we received a letter from aunt Maimaine in Switzerland. She told us that the Sarthe had been liberated in August by American troops commanded by General Patton and that our parents were alive and well. Le Mesnil had been miraculously saved, practically at the last minute, by a German officer who had disobeyed orders when retreating and had not blown it up, although the cellars had been carefully mined for that purpose. She also told us that her daughter, our cousin Ivy, had just given birth to a little boy, and both were well. Then very sad news: our cousin François de Boislisle, over whose head I had once emptied a jug of cold water, had been killed in action.

She ended her letter saying she hoped that we would all be reunited in 1945 and sent her fondest love. Shortly after receiving our aunt's letter we left Sunnyside for good. Driving away in the local taxi with my little bag containing my diary, photos and clothes, I sighed with relief and did not look back.

WALLY FOUND A SMALL FLAT in Bayview, Abbeyside—near Dungarvan. There Biddy and I shared the front sitting room in which there was a narrow bed. Wally and Marguerite shared the small bedroom. I was delighted because the kitchen had a tap with cold running water and the lavatory was not outside.

The technical school was just over the bridge on the other side of town. I had to cross the bridge, pass in front of the cinema and the Devonshire Arms Hotel, then walk around the square by the post office and most of Dungarvan's shops. On the far corner was a wide street that led me straight to the Tech. It was wonderful, only half a mile at most, so when it rained I didn't get completely wet. Another good point was that I had more time to study and could even have a piano lesson once a week with Miss Delaney. Things were improving in our little world as they were in the world at large. Grand-maman sent Wally extra money and, to my surprise, she let me keep five dollars from uncle Dick.

In the middle of November a telegram arrived from Scotland addressed to me. It gave me goosebumps and Wally stared at me wide-eyed as I opened it.

Send telephone number to this address stop
will call nine p.m. Friday
Richard Raoul-Duval.

I went at once to the post office and sent him the telephone number of the Devonshire Arms Hotel. On Friday shortly before nine we went there with Wally. We were silent, lost in our own thoughts, waiting. We didn't remember ever having seen our mother's brother, Uncle Richard. All we knew was that he was Aunt Sylvia's husband and that they lived in California and had three children. He was in the American Army. (In fact, he was with the OSS but we did not know it at the time.) I was trembling slightly. For the first time in over four years I was going to hear the voice of a member of my family, even if only briefly, since wartime calls never lasted more than three minutes.

"We are not going to be waifs much longer," I said to my sister, who seemed not to know what to think.

That night we waited at the hotel until midnight. Uncle Richard didn't call. Wally was fit to be tied and muttered unpleasant things all the way back to Bayview. Marguerite and I were silent.

Ten days later a second telegram arrived:

> Will call at nine tonight stop.
> Uncle Richard

Once again, we went to the hotel and waited. At ten o'clock the phone rang at last. It was for us. I was startled by my uncle's American accent. I couldn't hear him very clearly; he seemed to be speaking from very far away. "I'm just back from France, I have seen your father and mother. They are both well and Le Mesnil is still standing." Tightly I held the phone to my ear, with Wally and Marguerite standing close to me. I was very nervous and close to tears. Nearly choking, I asked him, because I wanted to hear it again, "How is Daddy and Mummy?" "Fine, just fine," said his quiet American voice, "and we are all making plans for your return to France as soon as possible."

He then spoke to Marguerite. Shaking so much she could barely hold the phone, all the poor child could manage was "yes, no" and a feeble "goodbye."

Then the line went dead. The three minutes were over. Wally had not spoken to our uncle. The phone call was over and Wally's face was a wrathful black. I thought she would strike me down right there in the hotel but she did not. I wondered what I had done wrong. On the walk home, she fumed mightily.

"How dare you, how dare you make a fool of me after all my kindness to you for so many years! What will your uncle think? How dare you say"—she mimicked my voice—'How is Daddy and Mummy?' You should have said 'How *are* Daddy and Mummy?' "

"It was the emotion."

"How dare you be emotional, you stupid fool!" was her answer. She was beside herself because she had not been

My cousin François de Boislisle, killed in action.

Uncle Richard Raoul-Duval, 2nd Lieutenant, U.S. Army, OSS.

able to speak to my uncle. I could understand what a terrible disappointment it was to her not to have spoken to an American war hero, a demigod in all our eyes.

DECEMBER 1944 WAS VERY COLD, with an icy wind, and Wally turned up one afternoon with a large parcel of secondhand clothes. We were very grateful. I had for years been stuffing folded newspapers under my sweater, one over my chest and another over my back to keep out the cold. As a personal joke, I preferred a summer edition of the *Irish Independent*. On the other hand, it was difficult to get rid of the smell in those secondhand clothes, and so despite their warmth, I disliked wearing them. Never, I vowed, when the war was over, would I wear smelly old clothes of unknown origin. I particularly remember hating my warm but ugly apple green coat that never had time to fully dry, so constant was the rain. No one had ever given us proper raincoats and the wool would become heavy with water and foul with another person's nasty smell. I didn't know where Wally found these clothes or who gave them to her and I hated them. Forever after I disliked secondhand clothes. Old clothes, if they had belonged to a friend or to me, I loved, but this distaste for the discarded clothes of strangers was one thing that stuck with me from these years. I have never minded eating the same frugal food every day. I still like potatoes, and for years avoided sweets, chocolate, cakes and meat. I still prefer margarine to butter. But the smell of unwashed, unknown bodies in those ratty wool clothes I can never forget.

In the middle of December a letter arrived for Wally from Mrs. Scrope. It was in fact a list of orders. Mrs. Scrope had received a letter from my mother and instructed Wally to contact the French legation in Dublin immediately to get our papers in order, so that we could leave Ireland as soon as possible, early in the new year. Mrs. Scrope did not bother with polite formulas either at the beginning or end of her letter. No longer used to taking orders, Wally was cross and shaken. But she wrote at once to the French legation, making a fuss about the injustice of it all, between bouts of sighs and tears. She suddenly seemed very old, and I found myself feeling sorry for her. Our lives were about to begin again, but she acted as though hers were ending. We were going home, and although I told Marguerite that over and over, I don't think she quite believed me and was rather frightened.

I do remember wondering why Wally had not written to the legation sooner. I had not even known it existed. Might they not have helped us earlier with other things? But given Wally's sudden misery, I said nothing.

The request for documents having been set in motion, Wally went looking for satisfaction from Mrs. Scrope, this untitled and pushy English stranger who had dared to treat her in a highhanded manner. She forwarded Mrs. Scrope's stern letter, along with a florid account of her own complaints, to Lady Waterford and soon an epistolary war was on between the three of them on how and when we would be returned to France. I was beginning to feel like a piece of furniture about to be shipped abroad.

Ten days later another letter arrived from Mrs. Scrope flatly asking Wally if she had done what she was told regarding the French legation and asking when our papers would be ready. She claimed that my mother had written saying that she was "furious with Sylvia who does not want to come back to France!" This time I was very upset, and could not understand who would tell my mother such a terrible thing. Who had told such a lie? After reflecting for several days, I finally determined that it must have been Wally. Of course I wanted to go home and so did my sister. Wally was totally silent when I confronted her, and this confirmed my suspicion.

For the Christmas holidays, Lady Waterford invited us to Curraghmore. My friend Blanche was going to be there and I was thrilled. Wally made an awful fuss, wailing that our last Christmas in Ireland should be spent together in our little flat in Abbeyside. With insidious skill, she brain-washed poor Marguerite, who gave in and announced that she would stay with Wally, who did not want to go to Cur-raghmore. When I staunchly refused to be bullied, she finally accepted that I should go alone.

"You can go for three days."

Lady Waterford sent for me and, feeling selfishly happy, I left with many recommendations from Wally about how to remain a "good Catholic" and be a "good example" in a Protestant house, and I promised to go to Mass on Christmas day with Winnie, Lady Waterford's sister, who had become a Catholic.

On Christmas eve I sat in the front of the car beside the friendly chauffeur. As he drove through the gate into the forecourt of Curraghmore I gazed happily at the beautiful Saint Hubert stag that surmounted the main entrance and reminded me so much of France.

That Christmas was the best that I had ever known. The war, we hoped, was nearly over. Adults and children alike were beginning to feel the burden on their shoulders lighten. Lady Waterford gave me a charming old fashioned bracelet—a simple chain with semiprecious stones of various colors that had been given to her when she was a young girl. I loved it. I had never had a bracelet before and I was overcome with gratitude. I was also sad because I was unable to give a single present, but no one seemed to notice.

After dinner the night before my return to Dungarvan, I went with Blanche to her room. It was late and we both sat on the carpet by the fire gazing into the flames, listening to the crackling wood.

"It's going to be wonderful after the war," said Blanche. "No more problems, we'll have great fun. I have lots of plans, but first I want to know what's the matter with you. Instead of being happy you are white faced and silent."

"I'm terrified," I blurted out, not knowing how really frightened I was until I heard myself say it. "I have night-mares all the time. I can only tell you, no one else would understand. I'm terrified at having parents again and worried about what I'll find. Wally once said I was unstable, and maybe it's true. Of course I'm happy but I also have a terrible sense of foreboding. The last time my parents saw me I was eleven years old and now I am sixteen! Perhaps they won't like me? Perhaps they will be disappointed in how I have turned out? We have grown and changed so much. I am certain that if we arrive in Paris with a lot of other children they won't recognize us—although I will recognize them."

"Don't be silly, they are your parents—they'll love you."

"I'm not sure—loving and liking are different. In any case they are going to get a shock. We're going to make them feel old."

Blanche thought for a moment. "All right," she said in a sensible matter-of-fact voice, "don't worry too much, and if you have problems with your parents, write to me. I have always had mine. They are not always easy and I know how to manage them. Just write to me and I will tell you how to deal with yours!" she smiled cheerfully. "Now tell me about your nightmares."

"I will tell you two. I am in the dining room at Le Mesnil. We are having dinner around the large oval table. I can see my mother and father and a lot of children that I don't know. They are not my cousins and yet they are calling my parents Uncle Jean and Aunt Elisabeth. These children are very polite, always agreeing with everything my parents say. Our parents are looking very happy with their large, unknown family. Then I try to talk and join in the conversation, but I can't. My mother talks a lot in a rather loud voice; my father is usually silent. I can see them—I'm sitting at the table—and yet they don't seem to be able to see me. Or they don't want to. I always wake up very upset."

"What is the other one?"

"My mother is organizing games. She has a big round ball and she wants all the children, including me, to play with it. I tell her that I cannot play, it's impossible; it's not my fault. I don't know how to play like that anymore—that part of me no longer exists. She is very cross. Then I go and get a book which makes her even more furious. She goes and plays with her ball and the children. They are waving and shouting, and she is bouncing up and down. . . . What do you think? Am I suffering from premonition?"

"You must stop worrying about nightmares that may never happen."

"Thank you, Blanche. You are a friend."

"Now let's get on with plans for after the war. First of all, I want to travel."

"Me too," I agree. "To Italy, to Greece and also to America."

"We'll have lots of parties. I will rent a house in Dublin for the Horse Show week. You must promise you'll come. It will be such fun—brave, good-looking men and fast horses."

"Nothing better," I smiled. "I promise to come. Brave men and lovely horses. One day I will organize a party in France. You must come to Le Mesnil."

"I promise. Do you want to ride tomorrow?" she asked.

"I would love to. Your aunt Winnie has lent me her jodhpurs, but they're too large. You must lend me a belt so that they don't fall down!"

"Here is an old one of mine. Keep it as a token of friendship. Now go to bed. I will wake you at seven. Goodnight."

"Goodnight," I answered, happily tiptoeing back to my room.

The next morning, we went riding with Tyrone. We followed him out of the long stables across the forecourt and rode down a narrow path to the fast flowing river Clodagh. We crossed over an arched medieval bridge, and onto a wider path. Tyrone cantered up the hill through thick woodland and we followed more tentatively. He rode beautifully, much better than we did, but we galloped along with him, out of the forest and over the hills and banks of

Curraghmore, following our fearless young leader, laughing bravely as the jumps became larger and wider. At times it seemed as if our horses were about to leave the fields and fly.

The next day, after thanking Lady Waterford for a wonderful Christmas, I went to say goodbye to my friends, passing through the beautiful blue dining room and up the staircase. I found Blanche, who said again, "Don't worry. If you have any problems with your parents or with anyone else, you can always write to me and I will always answer. Good luck and Happy New Year."

"Good luck, and Happy New Year to you as well." We gave each other a hug as we parted.

After the war, Blanche made good on her promise and gave a splendid Horse Show party in Dublin which I was unable to attend. Shortly after she was killed in a motor car accident.

My passport.

CHAPTER EIGHT

Diary

O N MONDAY, THE FIRST DAY OF JANUARY 1945, I
started my new diary. It is a small book with a hard
black cover. I don't want to forget the things that will happen in the weeks and months to come and so I decide to
write at least a little every day. My thoughts are tumultuous,
but my schoolgirl handwriting remains neat and precise.

The new year started quietly. I went to eight o'clock
Mass in the morning at the Priory. I had breakfast and
helped with the housework. I wrote goodbye letters to Lady
Granard, Jean Miller, Mary Daly, Lady Dawnay, Teresa
and Mark Girouard. We had a piece of turkey for lunch, the
first in years, and it was delicious! The war news is improving; the Germans are getting it good and hard. I hope 1945
will see the end of this horrid war.

In the afternoon I took a walk with Lorna Siberry. She
is very sweet but does not read enough and my mind wandered. I am extremely preoccupied. I spent the evening
practicing the piano.

The following day the weather is terribly cold with an
icy wind, it is "the coldest winter they can remember" say
the old people of Dungarvan. In bed I wear woolly socks
and a woolen cap on my head. I keep my underclothes on
under my nightie and spread my green overcoat on top of
my blanket. Wally has a bad pain near her heart, and I hope
that it isn't serious. I am furious with Marguerite. Even

now that Wally is unwell, my sister never helps with the housework and does not even keep her own things tidy. She actually sits by the window doing nothing. I am afraid that she is lazy, or perhaps she is ill, although she looks perfectly healthy.

Jan. 4. The postman has brought us two letters. One is from the Irish permit office regarding the special document we need to leave Ireland. I wonder if we will ever actually embark, we need so many different papers. The other is a long and loving letter from Grand-Maman, who has received good news of both uncle Richard and uncle Gerry. They are in active service, one with the OSS, the other with General de Gaulle. Grand-Maman makes me feel that I have a family. I long to see her again and am sad that California is so far away.

I have written more letters today, darned stockings and studied *mon Français*. I have borrowed a French school-book which I read slowly aloud to myself. I keep busy learning the verbs and writing out the words to memorize the correct spelling. I am enormously relieved to discover that it comes back to me fairly easily.

It is too cold to go out, so I practice the piano, wearing my coat all the while. Mai has invited me to the pictures to-morrow. She really is such a good friend, and I will miss her when I leave. I do hope that one day it will be possible for her to come to Le Mesnil. I now seldom see Tony Lawn. He is always very kind but I find that he takes himself too seriously and does not have much of a sense of humor.

Before going to the pictures with Mai, I wrote to Grand-Maman and aunt Agnes Albert, who lives in San Francisco and is the wife of our German cousin. Wally's pain is much better, thank God.

News came over the radio at nine this evening that rail and sea communications for civilians between London and Paris will be reestablished on January 15th. I am so excited that I can think of nothing else.

The next day I go to Mass to thank God and then fill in

more official papers. They are not difficult to do. I show them to Wally and mail them the same day.

We start breaking up the flat on Saturday, giving back things that were lent to us. We will stay at the Devonshire Arms until we leave. Miss Ryan, at the hotel, has the flu, I hope I don't catch it.

I study French and try to coax Marguerite into joining me, but I have no success. She has become very stubborn. Now thirteen years old, she can barely read or write. She speaks not a word of French and can neither sew nor knit. She should have been sent to school. Wally has always treated her like a small child, even making her bed, and this has spoiled her in a way. Studying alone is not easy, but I forge ahead. I don't want my parents to find me too ignorant, and it is very exciting to retrieve what I thought was forgotten for good.

I don't return to Tech on Monday. Instead I go for a bicycle ride with Lorna. During our ride, I ask if she knows Mr. and Mrs. Walsh, who have a large property, and I tell her that Mr. Walsh is Wally's brother and that we have never met him or his family. Now that we hope we will be going to France soon, I would like to meet him to say "thank you," as he has quite often given us butter.

"Yes," said Lorna, "I don't know them personally but I know who they are. They have a farm and a lot of children. They are very nice people—everybody likes them—and they work very hard and are famous for the quality of their butter."

At last I understand why Wally hasn't wanted us to meet her brother. She is so proud and has always said that her family was descended from the Kings of Ireland. She would have preferred her brother to be penniless gentry than an honest and hardworking, comfortably off farmer. Her reasoning is beyond me and I cannot understand such a stupid lie.

Later in the day, I see Mai Flaherty. She is going to a Children of Mary's party at the convent this evening and says that good-looking Mick Connors is in town, but we haven't seen him.

As days go by, I am really getting quite "holy." I would never have believed it. I am so grateful that the war is nearly over, that our parents are alive and that we are going back to France that I thank God all the time and go to Mass every morning. I find that praying calms me and make a habit of going to the earliest Mass, since it never has a sermon to spoil things.

At last we are back at the hotel. Dr. McCarthy has just seen Miss Ryan, who does have the flu, and he says we're all going to get it.

I am tired from packing, unpacking and moving heavy things, so I spend the evening reading detective stories by a little fire. Books are still my escape. Then to bed where I write in my dear little diary. The hotel is not heated and my room is icy cold.

Tomorrow I will go back to the flat with Wally to finish tidying up. Marguerite as usual manages not to come with us or help in any way. If she was more energetic she would perhaps be happier and not spend so much time alone playing with her dolls. I hope that she's not ill. Later in the day I see Lorna. She has had a perm and Wally has gotten it into her head that we should too. I can't imagine why. Marguerite's hair is already wavy—mine of course is long, silky and dead straight. Wally says that straight hair is ugly and unfashionable, and she is going to talk to the hairdresser and make an appointment. I don't know what to do. I don't want to set Wally off, but would really prefer to keep my hair the way it is, the way I can manage it myself.

Wednesday, Jan. 10. This morning Wally has received a most outrageous letter from Mrs. Scrope. She is fit to be tied. Mrs. Scrope says that she has written to Daddy and Mummy saying that we don't want to go home. This time I have written to her myself (for the first time) to say that it is not true, that we are longing to go home. How could she write such a thing? I ask. My letter is polite but not friendly: I am too upset. Also, I cannot understand why the horrible

Mrs. Scrope talks about us as if we were pieces of furniture to be transported "carefully labeled" and "carriage paid." She also says that it is most unlikely that Wally will be able to travel with us. At this piece of news Wally completely loses her composure. Spluttering mad, she keeps repeating that it is her "absolute duty" to "see us back" to our parents. She promises to post my letter to Mrs. Scrope.

I think that Wally is worried because she doesn't yet know where she will live when we leave if she is not allowed to come with us. I don't know what I can do to help. Adults are quite impossible.

Marguerite has had her hair permed. It looks all right. I saw Kathleen Carroll today, who is very nice and "crackers" about Mick Connors. And I saw Mai, who invited me to the pictures. She is suffering from "lovitis," poor thing. That has not yet happened to me and I am in no hurry. I decide to go to bed early, as I want to get up at the break of dawn tomorrow. I do, and watching the sun rise from the bridge was simply marvelous, and true to its promise, the whole day was beautiful.

Wally has received a letter from Lady Waterford and has telephoned her. She tells me that Lady Waterford does not understand Mrs. Scrope. I find it difficult to understand what is going on, and I hate to think of them fighting, and they really are fighting! Don't we all want the same thing? It is very upsetting and I am beginning to wonder if Wally isn't trying to hang on to us, poor old sausage.

Jan. 15. This afternoon, I had a raging headache, so I went for a walk by the sea. Later I met up with Mai, Kathleen and some other kids. Joe asked me if there was anything that I wanted to do before leaving Dungarvan. "Yes," I said, "I would like to go back to Clonea Strand, find a horse, and gallop from one end of the beach to the other." I had often thought that I would love to do that. He said that he would try to arrange it, but I think it highly unlikely that Joe can find two horses.

However, the next afternoon Joe comes to our hotel and says that he has found a farmer who will lend us two horses next Sunday. I am delighted and accept. We decide to keep it a secret, even though more and more Wally lets me do what I want. She cries a lot. It is terribly upsetting, especially as there is nothing I can do about bringing her back to France with us. It is she who is now an alien, and she doesn't like it at all. "Be patient," I tell her. "My parents will certainly look after you financially." But she doesn't listen to me, and I leave her to her crying.

That same evening Marguerite and I escaped from Wally and went for the first time to an Irish dancing class where we learned "The Walls of Limerick." Later I studied French and the piano.

The following Sunday was a wonderful day. I met Joe after lunch and we bicycled out to Clonea Strand. We left our bicycles against the wall of the hotel, which has closed for the winter. I waited there while Joe went to get the horses. I was afraid the farmer might have changed his mind, but soon Joe, a good-looking lad, was back with two horses of about the same size, with bridles but no saddles. They had kind faces and seemed quiet. Using the low wall we scrambled onto their backs. My horse was a dark bay, Joe's a chestnut. We walked to the far end of the beach near the dark rocks. The tide was low and the weather lovely with a slight breeze.

"Let's have a race," I suggested.

"What will be the prize?" asked Joe.

"I don't know."

"A kiss?"

"Why not?" I laughed.

Together we checked our horses and said "One, two, three, go!"

We raced along the flat beach. I grasped my horse's thick mane with all my strength. It was exciting, but I was a little afraid of falling off, never having raced without a saddle or stirrups. Joe won the race, and got his kiss.

After walking our horses along the beach in the low waves to cool them down, it was time for Joe to return the horses to the farm.

While I waited for him, sitting on the shingle, I played my harmonica. Soon I heard Joe's pleasant Irish voice singing along with my favorite Irish melody, "The Hummingbird." Accompanied by my little harmonica and the mighty Atlantic Ocean, Joe sang. I like Joe because he is kind and, like me, loves to ride horses.

That evening I had a bath; the water was grand and hot. I felt tired and my muscles were a little stiff. Lady Waterford phoned Wally. She was just back from Dublin, where she had seen Monsieur Sauvage at the French legation. He said he was sure that we could get home in February. I hoped that he was right.

Talked to Kathleen Carroll this morning. She has done a French composition in a great hurry. I arranged it a bit for her. She has very childish handwriting. I like her very much but I don't want to have any more close friends. We're leaving soon, and leaving friends is too sad.

There is a market fair in Dungarvan today, a small one with few animals because there now is "foot and mouth" disease in England. Kind Lady Waterford has sent us some firewood and a letter from Mummy to John Silcock, a friend of Lady Waterford's, on leave, who had contacted our parents while fighting in France. It is a very cool letter, nearly rude, not nice at all. I wonder why? I am very worried because I do not understand why Mummy is unkind to people who have tried to look after us and have been very kind to us for so many years and whom she has never met.

I stayed in bed all day with a bad cold. The weather is very windy and rainy, so I don't mind being in bed. I read. Wally has written a long letter to Grand-Maman in California telling her all about our difficulties with Mrs. Scrope and Mummy's "cold and unfriendly" letters. I feel that whatever the "difficulties," I will be heartbroken if we do not travel on February 10th. Now that boats are going with civilians and business people we must go; the suspense is frightful. We must go in February, but everything seems to be such a muddle.

After two days in bed, my cold was better although my nose was still very red. I got up and sat by the fire downstairs reading a detective story. In the afternoon Mr. and Mrs. Walsh came to see us. Wally was none too pleased, and received them in our upstairs sitting room. I looked at them with interest and curiosity and I thought that they looked very kind. They brought us each a present. Mine was a pretty Irish brooch and Marguerite's a bracelet. We sat around the table but Wally didn't order tea. This really astonished me as I knew that in Ireland everyone is always offered a cup of tea.

Wally was silent and smoked her cigarettes. Mr. Walsh asked me a few questions about our journey and I replied as clearly as possible, although in fact the details weren't too clear even to me. Then Mrs. Walsh said to Marguerite, "You will be so happy, dearie, to see your Mummy and Daddy again!" To which my sister replied, "To be sure I'll be happy to see them again, but I don't know what they look like anymore." Then Mr. Walsh said to his sister, "Kathy, those girls look very sensible to me, and not 'wild as two march hares,' the way you always said." They kissed us both goodbye and wished us a safe journey, then gave Wally a cool nod and left. I was so sorry not to have met them sooner, they seemed so warmhearted and kind. I also thought that it must not be easy to have a sister as complicated as Wally.

Uncle Dick has sent me a belated Christmas present and a very welcome five dollar check. There was a heavy fall of snow last night and this morning I watched several snowball fights from my window. The children are having a great time, as it seldom snows in Ireland.

I also received another letter from Grand-Maman, our only sensible relative. I hope she lives for a long time, otherwise God help us. Mummy says that she has moved "heaven and earth" to get us back in February. Wally says, "If she had not dumped you years ago in Ireland with no money, all of this would never have happened." I understand her point of view and am beginning to wonder what my parents are really like; I only have a child's memory of them.

To keep my mind off my foreboding, I spent the morning doing French verbs, then went with Wally to buy a length of tweed for a coat for Mummy with Grand-Maman's check.

Wally has arranged a lace collar given to me by Miss Ryan on my new blue dress, which has been bought in anticipation of our journey. It is very pretty, and I am grateful to them both. I telephoned the French legation and spoke in French for the first time in years. I was delighted to be understood. Our papers are ready. We haven't received them yet because they have been sent to Wally's brother's home address, and that is the reason for the delay. We had feared them lost.

I slept badly. I have the jitters at the thought of meeting my family. I am suffering from a lack of confidence, in myself and certainly in others.

It rained and then it froze last night and the whole town is like a frozen lake with tipsy people trying to walk and falling down on their derrières.

This evening Tony Lawn, Joe Riordan and Joe Foley came as a group to the hotel to say goodbye and wish us luck.

Thursday, 1st of Feb. Our papers arrived. It has taken a full week for them to find us. Wally is highly indignant with the Irish postal service. There is also a letter for Wally from Mummy, brought to Dublin by Monsieur Rivière, the new French minister to Eire. This letter, although icy, is not as rude as the previous one. Wally was cheered a bit. I am very sad because I have never seen my father's handwriting, not a single letter. I wonder why? I have written to him.

We received a cable from Grand-Maman and more money. I went out for the first time in days, saw Mai and had a pleasant day. Wally, who was not very worldly, her employers having always arranged these things in the past, suddenly realized that we had no sailing tickets to cross the Irish Sea to England.

"What shall we do, Sylvia?"

Wally is at a loss, but a thought comes to me. Mr. Siberry, I will talk to Mr. Siberry, he is such a nice man. He runs the hardware store where I buy the batteries for my torch, to read by. Mr. Siberry phones his son Ivor in Dublin at once. It is settled then. Ivor will buy our tickets and send them to us. That is a relief.

A letter from Lady Waterford tells us that there is a lot of snow at Curraghmore and that she and her sons will cross to England with us. Mines and German submarines make it still very dangerous to cross the Irish Sea or the Channel. I am writing goodbye letters—studying French—I have a terrible headache and did not sleep last night. More snow today. I went to my piano lesson. There is another dance tonight, and I wish I could go. But alas, Wally will not allow that, even if she is getting less strict. I go to confession instead. Life is not amusing.

I received two awful letters. I really cannot understand Mrs. Scrope or what is worse, my own mother. They seem to be upsetting Wally on purpose.

I am really getting very holy, indeed. I went to eight o'clock Mass, then spent the afternoon with Mai. Lars Foley bought a French newspaper in Dublin and gave it to me. I can read and understand it perfectly, which makes me very happy.

I wrote to uncle Dick to say "thank you" for his check. And I received a letter from His Excellency Monsieur le Ministre Rivière with an invitation for lunch or dinner when we go to Dublin en route for England. Now I do not doubt anymore that at last we are on our way home.

A T LONG LAST, a wonderful letter from my father has arrived. He says that he cannot wait to see me again and hopes that I still remember how to ride. I keep his letter in

FOREIGN OFFICE

Telephone : WHITEHALL 9060.

Telegraphic Address : "TELPASOF PARL, LONDON."

Please quote *Reference,* ....

C 183

The Director of the Passport and Permit Office presents his compliments to **Miss. S. Couturie** and has to inform **her** that a place (Travel Serial Number **C-184** Class **1st** on boat) has been allotted to **her** for the service to Paris on **14. February 1945**. The train will leave Victoria Station at **08.00** and the scheduled arrival time in Paris is **22.00.**

Rail and sea travel tickets will be obtainable only from the Continental Enquiry Office, Southern Railway, Victoria Station, S.W.1. Personal application should be made between the hours of 8 a.m. and 6 p.m. Outside these hours the office will be open earlier or later according to the train departure time, but only for the issue of tickets for travel by that particular train.

Applicants will be required to establish their identity, and to give the Serial Number of the passage allocated to them (as notified by the sponsoring Department).

Only single tickets for the through journey from London to Paris will be issued, and no break of journey at the French port or at intermediate stations will be permitted.

Persons allotted 1st or 3rd class on ship may elect to travel 1st, 2nd or 3rd class on the railway sections of the journey.

This letter should be produced when booking tickets.

My exit document from the British Foreign Office.

Marguerite and me dressed in our best clothes, including new shoes, for a visit to Curraghmore.

my pocket and carry it with me all the time. I am absolutely beside myself with joy. A burden of doubt has been lifted. But Marguerite seems to be in a complete daze—it's all too much for her.

Wally has received a letter from Lady Waterford. Enclosed is quite a polite note to Lady Waterford from Mrs. Scrope putting all the blame on Wally and me. Wally is livid and calls all the saints in Ireland down on the head of Mrs. Scrope. I can't understand what I could possibly have done wrong, but apparently I am somehow to blame for not organizing our journey quickly enough. I am terrified and indignant that my mother may be angry with me. I can't figure any of it out. I have raging headaches.

Today we went to Curraghmore. Our papers and tickets are finally in order and we will travel from Ireland to England with Lady Waterford, who is taking Tyrone and Patrick to boarding school. Mr. Siberry has arranged our tickets. I am delighted.

The next day, wearing our new clothes, we went to Clonmel with Mr. Harty in Mr. McCarthy's car to say goodbye to our friends there. Mr. Fennessy gave us each a pair of new shoes in real leather. We had lunch at the Kellehers'. Frances showed us her new frock. They said that they will miss us in Clonea next summer. We called at Moores', Dwyers', Moroneys' and Mulcahys'. They are all very nice and seem genuinely sorry to see us go. Frances gave me a pretty brooch.

We had never been in Clonmel before; it is a pretty little town. On the way back Mr. Harty drove us to Hannabul's to see the horses. We saw one belonging to Baron de Rothschild, one that was going to Brazil, another to India and several to France. Mr. Harty has a brother in the RAF, an officer in Yorkshire.

I am feeling very tired and my handwriting in my diary is going all jerky and ugly—I wonder why? I am not able to control my pen. This, and I did not know it then, was a sign of stress and depression.

It rained all day. I wrote letters and darned old stockings to go with my new shoes. A big dance is going on in the town hall, and a lot of my friends are there. Mai dropped in on her way—she looked fabulous with her black hair clasped to one side with a comb, Spanish style, with bright red lipstick and gold earrings to set off her dark complexion. She had poured half a bottle of scent over herself and would not go unnoticed at the dance. When she left I had a bath and went to bed. No dancing for me.

This morning I had my last music lesson. Miss Delaney gave me a box of chocolates and two letters for friends of hers in France which she asked me to post when I get home.

Feb. 2nd. Our passports arrived safely this afternoon, with the appropriate visas, all in order for France. Our photos look a little unreal as we have both changed a lot. I have to assure Marguerite that they will know it is her.

We went to Clonea to say goodbye to Johnny and Johanna, bringing them gifts of chocolate, sugar and tea. They were sad to see us go and they both cried, which surprised me. We also went to say goodbye to Mrs. Monahan at the hotel, who gave us each a box of lovely Irish embroidered hankies. I will keep mine for Grand-Maman. I saw Mai, who reported that the dance last night was a great success. Tony Lawn was there but not Mick Connors, so several girls were disappointed. Mai told me that she thought that Mick had a crush on me and I feel quite grown up, but do not really believe her.

Every day there are more "goodbyes," and I am getting fed up with them. Chocolates seem to be the parting gift of choice, and since I do not care for them, I give them to Wally. We start to pack. We have strict instructions to carry only one suitcase apiece, but that isn't difficult, since we don't have much anyway—and yet I am very sad to leave behind the few books I own and love.

Wally cries all the time and it upsets me. I hate to see people cry, and I try to comfort her by buying her a new pair of gloves, but it does little good.

Finally, I gave in to Wally's urgings and went to have my hair cut and permed. If this is the fashion, then so be it.

It took hours to do and the result is horrible. As it was Wally's idea, she says it is very pretty.

I find that I no longer look like myself. The hotel staff got together and gave us two more boxes of chocolates and so did Miss Dunne. I couldn't help but think that all this kindness might have done us more good before we were getting ready to leave, but they seemed so sad to see us go that I remained silent.

Mick Connors asked me to go to the pictures with him tomorrow afternoon. I said yes. He is really quite good looking and has no pimples. I won't tell Wally and just hope she doesn't find out before we leave.

SUNDAY, THE 4TH OF FEBRUARY, is our last day in Dungarvan. I go for a long walk with Mai and her little cousin in his pram. It rains and my hair starts to frizzle. I say "goodbye" to Mai, and we are both very sad. I lay awake the whole night.

The next morning at eleven Mr. McCarthy comes with his car and puts our two battered suitcases into it. My favorite books are too heavy to carry; they will have to follow us later. In the end they are lost or stolen and I never see them again. I take my autograph book and my diaries with me.

We are driven down to the barracks to say goodbye to the guards. The sun is shining and the whole countryside looks bright. We stop at Whitfield Court to say goodbye to Lady Susan Dawnay and don't reach the small city of Waterford until one o'clock. After lunch at the Savoy we go shopping for stockings and knickers. We take the four o'clock train to Dublin and I sit by the window. The countryside looks very much like County Waterford except that as we approach Dublin the mountains are higher. We arrive a little before nine, tired and dirty.

We go to Powers Hotel in Kildare Street. Marguerite

goes to bed immediately after supper but I stay up talking to Wally's sister Madge, who has agreed to keep our dog, Biddy. At last, at midnight, I go to bed. I am oh, so very tired. Tomorrow Wally has promised to take me shopping.

The shops in general are much more interesting than the ones in Dungarvan. Dublin seems a pleasant city and I recognize it a little from books I have read. There are trams and cars on the streets, more than I have ever seen in one place in Ireland. We are to meet Lady Waterford and her sons in Dunlaoghaire on Thursday evening. Mrs. Scrope has sent Wally and me a very kind letter. She is really odd. Wally took me to have my hair washed and set. It looks awful. I am very tired, but my handwriting in my diary is a little better today. Tomorrow we are invited by the French minister for lunch at the legation.

The next day Marguerite and I dress carefully in our new clothes. I shine my new shoes, spitting on a piece of newspaper and rubbing hard. I have never had lunch with a French minister before. We leave our hotel by taxi at half past twelve. We arrive at 53 Ailesbury Road promptly at a quarter to one and are shown into a large drawing room. There we meet Monsieur and Madame Rivière and their daughter. Using few words, I manage to answer questions in French. Marguerite doesn't utter a sound—she just nods her head. A door opens and a butler comes to tell Madame Rivière that lunch is ready. We go into a dining room with a large bay window. There isn't much conversation. We start lunch with hors d'oeuvres and then have delicious roast meat with vegetables. I recognize green peas and take a rather generous helping, seeing that Marguerite does the same. The butler pours some red wine into my glass, and since I'm thirsty I finish my glass easily. Just as I put down my glass I see that my sister is having a serious problem with her green peas.

An overly energetic movement with her knife has sent most of them off her plate to roll over the polished table and onto the carpet. She looks to Wally, who is glaring fiercely at her. Marguerite blinks her eyes, gets off her chair and disappears under the table after her peas. "Ce n'est pas grave (It is not important)," says Madame Rivière kindly as my sister returns to her seat.

I have a silent giggle as my glass is refilled with the delicious wine. I am sipping it happily when I see that Wally has now fixed her gimlet eye on me. Secretly amused, I put down my empty glass.

Monsieur Rivière tells Wally that he will help her get her own papers after Easter, when he thinks that she will be able to travel to France. We don't stay long after lunch. As soon as our coffee cups are empty we say "Au revoir et merci beaucoup (goodbye and thank you very much)" and leave.

Wally is very cross with us—we have both "disgraced" her. I am surely going to be an alcoholic and Marguerite is not fit for decent society. I don't pay much attention to her. That evening I am so tired that I sleep right through the night. Upon waking in the morning I realize that this is our last day in Ireland.

Wally and I again tour the shops, but she hardly looks and stops only for cigarettes which are difficult to find. She is very depressed. I know that my grandmother has sent her quite a lot of money and that she is going to live with her sister Madge, so I am not too worried about her immediate future. It is clear, however, that she has lost the focus of her life and is at loose ends.

We have lunch at Powers Hotel with Marguerite and Madge, who is a very kind woman, and I am pleased that Wally and Biddy will have a happy home at Gerardstown. At three o'clock we leave Dublin for Dunlaoghaire, where we will stay at the Real-Na-Mara Hotel. I go for a walk on the pier and admire the lovely little town.

The Waterfords arrived at seven that evening. The boys are wildly excited, their mother is as pleasant as can be, and we all have a cheerful dinner together, except for Wally who says little and has a dour look on her face. Before bed she resignedly tells us that she is sorry to see us go, but that at last she will at least be able to have a good rest. When she leaves us I wonder, not for the first time, how old she is. She would never say.

Precisely at six o'clock I am awakened by a loud knock. I am more surprised that I was able to sleep at all than I am startled at being woken. I dress in haste and go down to breakfast with the Waterfords. The porters are half asleep and we have a hard job boarding the small, sturdy ship. The customs officers are very respectful and do not open our luggage.

Wally sticks close to us right up to the gangway. It is quite awful having to say goodbye and I can't think of what to say. Wally is crying hysterically, and Marguerite joins in. I give Wally a quick hug and mumble goodbye. Thankfully we are herded rapidly up onto the deck and the gangway is quickly pulled back. Our ship pulls out of the port and I don't shed a single tear as I watch Ireland and Wally disappear into the Celtic mist.

The front part of Le Mesnil as seen from the avenue.

CHAPTER NINE

Home

W E ALL HAVE TO WEAR "MAE WESTS" during the whole of the journey because of the danger of sea mines and German submarines. The Mae Wests are very disagreeable and stink of old vomit. The sea is rough, with short hard waves. I try not to think of the German submarines, or the sea mines, remembering the explosions off the coast of Clonea Strand that shot water into the air as high as the Eiffel Tower in Paris.

Life is unfair. Lady Waterford, Marguerite and Patrick don't get sick at all. I throw up four times and Tyrone once. We stay on deck the whole trip, so we can be sick right into the sea. Tyrone is kind and teases me about "feeding fish." We both recover by the time we reach Holyhead, having safely crossed the Irish Sea. As soon as we enter port, I get rid of my stinking Mae West. There is a lot of noise: men shouting orders, the gangplank clattering down. "Soon," I think, "I will be in England." It does not take long for the small number of passengers to disembark. We stick close together as we leave the ship and are surrounded by cheerful and helpful porters who carry our suitcases and call us "Luv." The customs officers don't ask us to open our luggage. We could have brought the tweed we'd bought for Mummy after all. We left it at the last minute because Wally insisted it would be confiscated. The officials clip our tickets and stamp our passports, and it is great fun. Everyone is very friendly and polite to Lady Waterford, and I discover it helps to have a title and be a Lady when traveling in wartime.

I am excited to be in England at last. We have lunch at the Railway Hotel in Holyhead. For dessert we eat delicious pancakes with real lemons, something we have not seen since before the war. The sea air has made us very hungry. Every other seat in the restaurant is occupied by men in smart uniforms—British, American, and Australian soldiers, airmen and sailors. I am enthralled by their youthful beauty. As I cannot sculpt or paint them, and I fear they may soon be dead, I engrave forever their images on my mind. An official comes to tell us that our train will soon be leaving. On the platform, more obliging porters help us climb into a clean first-class carriage which we have all to ourselves. There are very few civilians and we are noisily cheered and waved off by all the military in the station together with the officials and porters. This, I think, is living. I enjoy every minute and stop having thoughts about death.

The journey to Crewe is slow. I keep my nose glued to the window, fascinated by all I see. There is such variety— drilling soldiers, airfields, English cottages, farmland, towns, trees . . . everything. It is dark when at last we arrive at our station. We get off the train and stand on the platform with our bags. A lady in a fur coat comes toward us. She has a yellow scarf on her head, a lot of makeup on her face and round spectacles on her nose. Lady Waterford looks at her, then says "Oh! Are you Mrs. Scrope?"

"Yes."

"Oh, this is Sylvia . . . Marguerite . . . my sons. I must go and see about our luggage." Lady Waterford disappears. After a few minutes chatting with Mrs. Scrope and a long silence, I go and look for Lady Waterford to help her.

There are many American soldiers around the luggage van. "These are the gentlemen you must be careful of," says Lady Waterford in a low voice. I think of Uncle Richard and wonder exactly what she means. Once the luggage has been sorted out, we have tea at the Crewe Arms Hotel. I send a wire to Wally to say that we have arrived safely. Mrs. Scrope pays for tea. There is not much conversation; both ladies are probably thinking of the disagreeable letters they exchanged in the recent past.

We are now headed in different directions, and Lady Waterford and the boys accompany us to our train. We are going north to Liverpool and they are going south to their boarding school. Tyrone and Patrick kiss us goodbye and both blush. I laugh and tease Patrick, whose face turns red. We keep hugging each other and saying "Good luck, good luck." We fondly kiss their mother, saying "Thank you, thank you for everything." She also is sad to say goodbye.

We climb into our train with Mrs. Scrope. At last it begins to move. Night has fallen and I cannot see anything outside of the train. Because of the blackout there is not a single lit window and England is as dark as the bottom of a coal mine. Instead I study Mrs. Scrope's face and decide that she looks like a kind owl. We converse a little. Marguerite has gone to sleep and I notice approvingly that Mrs. Scrope, with capable maternal hands, settles her more comfortably without waking her.

WE ARRIVE IN LIVERPOOL. We are met by Lord Derby's chauffeur in a huge car with a coat of arms and a coronet on each door. We travel in state to Knowsley. Because of air raids the lights of the car have been kept very dim and the chauffeur drives very slowly. It is only when we stop in front of the main door of the house and I see a single ray of light that I get my first vague sense of its overwhelming bulk.

Lady Derby is waiting for us by a fire in the library. She kisses us both and then shows us our rooms. She is a charming old lady, unfortunately a little deaf.

We have a hot bath and put on clean clothes for dinner. Mrs. Scrope knocks on my door. "Are you ready?" "Yes." Together we go to a drawing room where we meet Lord

Derby. He has not changed since I saw him at Le Mesnil. He is still very plump and has the same merry blue eyes. He is charming and delighted to see us again after so many years.

Marguerite and I are very shy. Our Irish brogue makes them smile a little, and their eyes fill with astonishment as they find out how we lived and how little education we have had.

The butler comes to say that dinner is served. We are only five at the table and I sit on Lord Derby's left, with Marguerite beside Lady Derby. After the green pea incident at the French legation, I keep an amused eye on her table manners. The dinner is delicious and rather formal. Lady Derby, who knows children's tastes, has thoughtfully ordered a chocolate mousse for dessert. As the youngest, Marguerite is served last, and she helps herself generously. A lot of mousse is left on the serving spoon, so she carefully licks the spoon before putting it back into the dish. The butler's face doesn't change; he goes to a side table and puts a clean spoon into what is left of the mousse. Later I notice Lady Derby signal him to pass the chocolate mousse a second time. When he comes to Marguerite my little sister looks up at him and in a clear voice and Dungarvan accent says, "No thank you, I have piles." At this remark the grown-ups collapse in laughter. We join in politely, although we don't understand the joke.

Then Lord Derby insists that we all drink a glass of champagne "in honor of our homeward journey and to glorious France." He also makes us promise to come back to see him after the war and Lady Derby says that she remembers Le Mesnil very well. I know I will never forget them, their kindness or my first glass of champagne.

At last it is time to go to bed. We say good night and Lord Derby tells me that he wants to see me alone in his library in the morning before we leave. Knowsley is huge, even larger than Curraghmore. Built over several centuries, in various architectural styles, one entire wing is reserved for the King and Queen when they come to stay. There are more windows than days in the year, a hundred bedrooms, six drawing rooms and seven libraries. That night we are taken to our rooms, which we would never have found by ourselves. Mine has an immense bed, big enough for five people. I feel tired and ever so small as I climb into its comfortable folds. On the walls hang three portraits of ancient ladies with long noses. One looks particularly sad.

I toss and turn and cannot get to sleep. I am too tired. I think of Wally and of Mai. The fire in the chimney is still burning, and I can clearly see the portraits. I sleep a little, then wake up. It is still night and there is a small glow from the fire. I look at the portraits and think that I see the sad lady smiling at me. "Why can't you sleep?" she seems to ask.

"I am worried about going back to parents that I do not know, and I'm afraid that they won't like me."

"You are not the only one to be worried about going home. Thousands of people are. There is no point in worrying—things always turn out differently from what we imagine. You will survive and I will watch over you tonight." The face that seemed alive once more becomes a portrait, and I fall asleep once again.

Early next morning a maid knocks on my door and enters with a breakfast tray. "Good morning, Miss, it's time to get up." She opens the curtains and says, "I'll come back for you in half an hour, Lord Derby is expecting you."

"Thank you," I say and quickly get dressed and eat my breakfast. I look at the sad ancient lady on the wall, and I want to thank her for her kindness. I remember that my harmonica is in my suitcase and quickly find it. I sit facing the portrait and play for her my favorite Irish song, "The Hummingbird." When I'm nearly finished, I glance at her and for a fleeting instant catch a smile in her eyes. I still have five minutes left before the maid comes, so I go back to the bathroom and gaze at my permed hair in the mirror. It is very ugly, so with my nail scissors I cut some off on each side of my face. Again, I hear a discreet knock on my door. "Are you ready, Miss?" I follow the maid along corridors and up and down stairs. At last we arrive.

"Come in. . . . Good morning, Sylvia dear. Please sit down," said Lord Derby, asking the maid to come back for me in five minutes.

"Did you sleep well?"

"Not very, I'm too excited."

"That's normal." There is a pause.

"I have a message for your father and only for him. You must wait until you are alone with him to give him my message. Do you have a good memory?"

"Yes."

"Good, you must tell him that I know for certain from secret military information that Monsieur X.Y. has been a collaborator and a traitor to his country. When the war is over he will be brought to trial and punished. You must tell your father from me that he must have absolutely nothing to do with this man. Will you remember this?"

"Yes, I will remember."

"What is his name?"

"Monsieur X.Y."

"Promise not to tell anyone else."

"I promise."

"Thank you and bon voyage. Now give me a kiss and off you go."

I give him a kiss and say, "Thank you for the money you sent us."

"That's all right. I only wish I had done more, now that I see . . . Now don't you worry. You're going to be fine—you're a good girl."

The maid arrives and takes me down to the main hall, where Lady Derby is talking to Mrs. Scrope. Marguerite is beside her and our luggage is already in the car. It is time to go; we do not want to miss our train. We say goodbye and receive another affectionate kiss.

WE LEAVE LIVERPOOL AT ELEVEN O'CLOCK on our way to Yorkshire. At Hull we change trains, and Mrs.

Scrope buys us each a banana. They are delicious, but Marguerite has forgotten about bananas and before I can stop her, she has bitten into the skin. She makes an awful face.

On the journey to Yorkshire we see many destroyed buildings. England has taken a terrible beating. At five in the evening we finally reach Nafferton and the Scrope family home, Wold House, which is quite large and built of brick. It even has its own chapel. We are totally exhausted so we take a hot bath at once, and Marguerite goes straight to bed after dinner. I stay up to telephone Lady Waterford. They have reached Penrrith safely and the boys love their school. At last I go to bed; I am very tired. I now write in my diary with a pencil as I have run out of ink.

Mrs. Scrope has six children of her own, and it is really very kind of her to look after us as well. The next day I have a good time playing with the Scrope children until lunchtime. Billums, the one I remember best, is a most enchanting little boy. After lunch we go back to Nafferton to pick up his sister Sally. She is physically quite different from her mother, with a long face and enormous blue eyes. She seems very wise and loves to laugh. She has just had the measles and has been in a nursing home with an ear infection. The five other children have whooping cough. It really was kind of their mother to come and get us at Crewe. Later, with Sally, we go into a field and make friends with horses. There she tells me that since 1939 the agricultural economy of the country has been left in the hands of the old men, the women and the children. She tells me what very hard work and what a fabulous job they have done. Sally, at age eleven, helped their Land Girl every day during her holidays. She would get up before dawn every morning to help wash the udders and hand milk thirty-five cows. At boarding school it was the children who harvested all the potatoes and apples. Although the work was tiring, most children were happy to help and proud of being responsible. I am very impressed.

Sally is a highly intelligent little girl and very amusing. We laugh a lot. I have no way of knowing on that lovely afternoon she will soon become terribly ill, first with double pneumonia and then with tuberculosis. Her vocabulary is enormous and amusing—a mix of erudite English, slang and horse stable swearing. She asks me about Ireland and I tell her about Wally and about her stupidity about Protestants. She listens carefully and then says, "She wasn't stupid, it was the way that she was brought up by the priests and the nuns. I have an aunt in Ireland, and she says they are all like that and that it is a great pity and makes for a lot of trouble, so Wally was not responsible." Later I think about what Sally told me, and feel a little sorry for having been so hard on Wally. But when Sally confirms my suspicion that Wally had done her best to delay our return to France, my sympathy evaporates.

On the following day Monsieur Leroi telephones just before lunch to say that all our papers are in order. We will sail early on Wednesday morning and reach Paris by eight or nine o'clock. We are to be escorted the whole way by Monsieur Malclaire, who is going to Paris. He is from the French legation in London. Later that day Mrs. Scrope receives a telegram telling her that our parents will be waiting for us at the station.

I am exhausted and increasingly nervous. I think it rather odd that I am not happier, but perhaps this is a good thing, especially if things do not turn out well. Marguerite has grown even quieter than usual, lost in her own misgivings. I would be less nervous if Grand-Maman was also going to be waiting for us in Paris, feeling that I know her better because of her letters from America, but she is still in California and will not be able to return until the war is over.

The evening before I left Wold House, Sally said, "I want to read you a funny story. It was in the newspaper and I cut it out." The Smithwick family near York had cousins in America who had sent them food parcels since the beginning of the war. In early December they received a large package containing the seventeen ingredients for a Christmas pudding, plus an unmarked container of powder. Mrs.

Smithwick mixed all of the ingredients together, including this year's new one, and steamed the pudding. On Christmas Day the whole family ate it. It was as delicious as ever, and they gratefully drank to their American cousins' health. In mid-January a letter arrived from the States:

Dear John and Mary,

Poor dear Uncle Peter died peacefully on the 20th of September. As he had always said that he wanted to be buried in England, we tried to send you his ashes by official channels but this proved so complicated that we decided to send them along with the Christmas pudding.

Thank you for putting him in our little plot in the cemetery near to the little church he loved so much. He was such a sweet man. We all loved him and he loved all of us so tenderly. We will miss him greatly. Happy Christmas and New Year to all of you.

With fondest love, Mark and Teresa.

On Thursday, the 13th of February, I got up early and with Mrs. Scrope and Marguerite went to the Hull Station Hotel, where we had breakfast. Afterward we took the train to King's Cross London where we arrived at two thirty that afternoon. I did not find the journey long, thanks to fascinating magazines that I had never seen before.

We went to the French consulate. Madame Abraham, a very beautiful woman who worked there, had sent all our papers to the embassy, so we had to go there to collect them, as well as our sailing tickets.

At the embassy we met Monsieur Leroi, a charming man who knew our uncle Gerry Raoul-Duval, our mother's younger brother and a French diplomat. Our uncle was well, he told us. He had fought in North Africa and in the battle of Bir Hakeim, where he had been by error reported killed in action. We then proceeded to Victoria Station where we left our luggage. We bought coffee to bring home with us, it being extremely scarce in France, and then went to the Norfolk Hotel where we spent the night.

"Our Scropey," as I now affectionately called her to myself, was behaving awfully well and was nothing like the monster Wally had thought her to be. I could only assume she had written those letters in reaction to Wally's efforts to hang on to us. I never did ask her about the letter I wrote to her and she didn't mention it. I think it likely Wally never posted it.

After supper we went to bed early, but not before I had another look at my hair. It was awful, so with my nail scissors I cut more of it off. Marguerite says I now look like a boy and that our parents will be very upset and cross. I am not happy about it myself. In fact, I rather mourn my long hair, having brushed it so often and having always thought that it was the prettiest thing I had, so I tell her to bloody well shut up and go to sleep.

Only one V2 rocket hit London that night. London is in a terrible mess. Many of the houses are empty shells and only a very few have any glass left in the windows. I cannot sleep. Later I hear men singing in French in the street, and I sing along with them a pretty tune, "Sur le parquet des vaches . . . ," a French Air Force song.

Driving in a taxi from station to embassy, then from embassy to another station and back to the hotel, I get a glimpse of Buckingham Palace and Hyde Park. How sad to see this beautiful city destroyed. It is heartbreaking.

At last, on the 14th of February, we sail. We get up at six and take the Underground to Victoria Station. We pace up and down beside our train, but there is no sign whatsoever of Monsieur Malclaire, our escort. Poor Scropey is getting frantic. At last she spots a respectable-looking middle-aged couple who look French, and dives into their carriage. She asks them if they are traveling to Paris. Can they please keep an eye on us? "Oui, certainement. (Yes. Certainly)." They are the Marquis and Marquise de Castellane. We barely have time to kiss our darling and efficient

Scropey goodbye before she has to leap off the train seconds before it leaves, nearly breaking her leg in a spectacular crash landing. I will never forget her kindness.

ALL OUR PAPERS AND MONEY ARE IN MY BAG. Marguerite and I travel to Newhaven solemnly sitting beside each other and have breakfast on the train—very salty kippers with black coffee—and I feel terribly grown up. We are the only children and we are surrounded by men and women in uniform. It is a little unnerving when they stare at us, some with wistful expressions. One officer, who may have a daughter who looks like Marguerite, comes and sits beside her with tears in his eyes. She let him hold her hand.

At Newhaven, we get off the train and go through customs with the Castellanes and their pile of large suitcases. I have learned about titles and customs agents, but this is again something new: Monsieur de Castellane is an important diplomat. We whisk right on through and board the ship.

The Castellanes are both charming. Madame de Castellane is wearing a very high and ugly hat that somewhat resembles the shiny black oil stove that used to keep us warm in Clonea Strand. I wish that my French was more fluent. I understand everything but can barely speak. However, we manage quite well when they speak French and I answer in English.

Once again, everyone has to wear smelly Mae Wests in case of mines or German submarines, but the sea journey is lovely even if it is frightening. It is a bright but icy cold winter's day. The ship is full of men wearing a great variety of uniforms. There is a small handful of civilians and my sister is the youngest on board. I am not seasick and remain on deck until noon. We have lunch with Monsieur and Madame de Castellane and they are very friendly and talkative. They speak a French so lovely in all it nuances that it makes me furious that I cannot do the same, and I answer their questions in English. The sun is shining and the tall white cliffs look beautiful. We land at Dieppe and I walk on French soil at last.

We have no trouble with customs and climb into a dirty old French train, where we share a compartment and have coffee, toast and jam together. No dinner is served, as we are expected to arrive in Paris by eight or nine o'clock.

We travel very slowly. Again I keep my nose glued to the window and see that many houses are in a terrible condition, even worse than in London. I realize that this is normal because in France there were also land battles and many cities have been both bombed from the air and shelled by cannons during the fighting. Many are totally destroyed. Nearly all the buildings are black, and it is truly awful. The fields are full of bomb craters near the railway track and yet people bravely smile and shrug their shoulders and say, "*C'est la guerre!*"

As the train slowly passes, people wave to us, making V signs and blowing kisses. In silence I listen to the train wheels. They are saying, "I am going home, I am going home, and my heart is full of fear, full of fear." As we near Paris, Marguerite asks me in an anxious voice if I will recognize our parents.

"Yes, certainly, but don't worry, they will recognize us," I say. She looks very pale and frightened. I am glad we are the only children on the train. Had there been fifty, I would not have been absolutely certain that our parents would have recognized us!

It is nearly ten when at last we arrive at the Gare du Nord, half hanging out of the train window. In the distance I see a couple standing closely together on the dark platform. The woman is taller than the man, and I recognize their silhouette, not their faces.

They see us and start to wave. The train stops. There is a great deal of noise. My head is filled with a loud and strange music and feels as if it is about to explode. In the corridor men in uniform stand to let us pass. Climbing over a mountain of military bags, we make our way to the nearest door, and when at last it opens we fall into the outstretched arms of our parents.

They hug and kiss us on the dark and freezing platform. We say goodbye and thank you to Monsieur and Madame de Castellane. A porter picks up our two suitcases and we proceed inside the station where there is very little light. Now our parents really stare at us, repeating, "You've grown . . . you've grown . . ." over and over. Our size seems to have given them a shock, and yet I know that we are of normal height for our ages and we have both become very thin during these last weeks. I have a huge lump in my throat and cannot speak. I look at my mother, who has barely changed and looks very healthy. My father has aged terribly. I have the feeling that something is missing, but what can it be?

My father tells us that Charles the chauffeur is waiting for us with the car. We move out of the main hall to the street. Charles hugs us both, though Marguerite barely remembers him. I remember that he drove us to Le Havre nearly five long years ago. The car has changed; it now has an odd furnace attached to its rear. My father sits in front with Charles; my mother sits in the back between my sister and me and we drive through empty streets to Grand-Maman's flat in rue Raynouard. We have to walk up the six flights of stairs because there is no electricity for the lift. I am dead tired—we have been up since six in the morning and it is now eleven at night. René and Jeanne who work for Grand-Maman are waiting for us and they are delighted to see us and give us both an affectionate kiss.

Our parents never share a bedroom because Papa snores, so I am going to sleep in his room in a narrow bed near the window and Marguerite is going to share Maman's room which also has two beds. As it is very late we get nothing to eat. I would have loved a hot drink and some bread but dare not ask and do not say that we had no supper on the train. Our parents do not seem to know much about children, as they do not even think to ask if we are hungry.

Paris seems almost as cold as Dungarvan. I use my coat as an extra cover on my bed, take off my shoes and skirt and slide in between the sheets, keeping my woolen bonnet on my head and my fists pushed into my stomach to keep off the hunger. A little later I hear my father getting into his bed. He says: "Good night, ma chérie, I will wake you at seven tomorrow," and then turns off the light.

After a few minutes I ask: "Papa, are we alone?"

"Yes, why do you ask?"

"Lord Derby has given me a message for you and you alone."

"Yes?"

"The message is that you must have absolutely nothing to do with Monsieur X.Y. He is a very bad man and a traitor to his country. He is going to be put on trial by the Allies as soon as the war is over. Lord Derby also said that he had a lot of information about him and that you must keep this message a secret."

"Thank you. I also know a lot about Monsieur X. Y., and I have never had anything to do with him. Good night, my darling."

I am dead tired and I can't sleep because I am so delighted to be home at last, yet something has happened to me that I cannot understand. When I am about to fall asleep I relax, and it is then that I know that psychologically part of me is now completely numb. This is perhaps the answer to the strange premonitions that frightened me so much during the past few weeks—that returning home would be very difficult.

A LITTLE BEFORE EIGHT THE NEXT MORNING I am looking at the strange contraption called a gasogene at the rear of my father's car. Charles is stocking it with charcoal and he explains to me that he must do this every hour and that it is this gas generator that makes the car move. I am fascinated. As we drive slowly through Paris sitting in the same seats as the night before, I keep my nose glued to the window and see that Paris has not been bombed in any way as much as London. I also think that I am dreaming when I see men on bicycles to which are attached little armchairs on wheels in which other men are sitting reading their newspapers. The drive to Le Mesnil is slow; signs of war are everywhere in the countryside.

I see lots of army lorries, tanks, ambulances, jeeps, fallen airplanes and great round holes made by the bombs that fell in the fields but that had been meant for the road. The beautiful Chartres Cathedral looks intact. My mother hugs us both and says, "You see how lucky you were, nice and safe in Ireland when all of this was going on . . ." I cannot answer because suddenly I hear the crashing waves of the Atlantic Ocean and bombs falling into the sea.

After three tire punctures, and just as the daylight is beginning to fade, the car turns right into our avenue with its double rows of plane trees on each side and at last I can see our home at the end of the avenue. My heart is throbbing in my throat. Then, in a voice that seems to be very far away, I hear my mother saying, "Oh, my darlings, I am so happy that there are two of you. Your daddy and I can have one each!" Little did she know that her words broke my heart. For years I had longed for parents—both a father and a mother.

A lot of people are in the hall to welcome us. When I see Mabel Smith I rush into her arms and kiss her dear old face over and over again. She doesn't say a word; she holds me tight, and to my delight I remember and recognize her odor.

Our rooms have been prepared; mine is next to my father's, Marguerite's next to my mother's at the end of the main corridor. The inside of the house is exactly the same as when we left. Outside the lawns have become potato fields.

At dinner we meet a lady I have never seen before. She

is staying at Le Mesnil. Her name is Madame de Cazotte and she has a very pretty figure and a band over one eye. Her husband is a prisoner of war in Germany and she is living at Le Mesnil because there is very little to eat in Paris and also she would be very lonely there. For dinner we have vegetable soup, rabbit with Jerusalem artichokes, and baked apples. I am so tired I can barely speak, and I go to bed early.

For the first time in weeks I sleep well and wake up just in time to get dressed and go down for lunch. Daddy and Mummy are both looking well and more relaxed. Jackie Decazes, the second son of our aunt Maimaine in Switzerland, and his wife Margarita have come for lunch. Margarita is of Spanish origin, and though not very tall, extremely beautiful with blue eyes and dark brown hair. I have never met her before. Jackie resembles his mother and is very tall, and they are clearly blissfully happy. They have just added a son to their family of two daughters, Marisol and Nadine. For the past four years they have lived in a little house in Savigné because it was safer than Paris and also much easier to get food. Le Mesnil was close for any other kind of help or support. They have invited me to tea tomorrow to meet their little Jacques-Marie and the girls.

As we sit around the large oval table I can hardly contain my happiness. It is so wonderful to have parents and cousins again. During this first meal at Le Mesnil we all speak English so that Marguerite can understand.

After lunch, Daddy, Mummy, Marguerite and I get into the pony trap and drive all around Le Mesnil. We go into every farm and cottage and say "Bonjour" to everyone we meet. There are three new people working in our house, including Madame La Bruyère and her daughter Mimi. Madame La Bruyère is Mummy's maid and she also looks after the linen. She is the wife of our huntsman and he now helps with the horses.

The third newcomer is André Fouquet. He is in his early twenties and has spent the last few years hiding in Touraine where he worked for the Comte and Comtesse de

Saint-Seine in a vast medieval château surrounded by lakes and a large forest. This was a very safe place to hide because the Château de Grillemont, like most old châteaux, has several secret rooms. André never went into a village or a town during these years because he didn't want to be caught by the Germans like so many young French men of his age and sent to work in forced labor in an ammunition factory in Germany.

After the liberation he came to Le Mesnil to work for my father, who had found him his safe hiding place. Now he looks after all my father's personal things, helps with the heavy work in the house and serves our meals in the dining room with Mimi, who is very graceful and pretty.

*T*HIS EVENING, OUR NEIGHBORS Monsieur and Madame Lescop are coming for dinner. At seven we all have a hot bath and change for dinner. At seven forty-five André gives three sharp strokes with a wooden stick on a round Chinese gong near the staircase to warn us not to be late for dinner. I put on my navy blue Dungarvan dress, my pretty Irish lace collar and Lady Waterford's bracelet. Our guests seem pleasant. Madame Lescop has a sweet smile and Monsieur Lescop never stops talking and asking questions. Everyone speaks only French. I understand every word but often cannot find my words fast enough to answer so I either nod my head up and down or shake it left and right. By the end of our meal my neck is quite stiff. My sister does the same but only up and down, which makes her look as if she agrees with everything that is said. Most people don't see that she doesn't understand a single word, but think how delightful she is since she agrees with everything they say.

We have a thick vegetable soup and rabbit for dinner, tonight with a mustard sauce, and afterwards we have pancakes with a little honey. Monsieur Lescop talks all the time. He asks me a lot of silly questions and doesn't listen to my answers. "Did you have a wonderful time in Ireland?"

"Did you have ponies, did you hunt?" I stare at him in round-eyed disbelief.

Then to my surprise he begins to tell me how fortunate we have been. "You are lucky girls because you know nothing about the war! You never heard planes or bombs. . . ! You always had a lot of delicious food. . . ! You were able to travel and visit all of Ireland, because Ireland is neutral . . . ! Yes, you are very lucky girls!"

Mummy is looking very happy and to my surprise agrees with everything Monsieur Lescop says. I find him stupid and pretentious. In Dungarvan they would have said he could talk "the hind leg off a donkey!"

At the other side of the table, Madame de Cazotte is smiling but not really listening. My father is listening and not smiling, in fact he is looking a little cross.

Carefully I venture more and more words in French but soon something strange happens to my jaw and the muscles around my mouth: they are sore from being made to move in an unaccustomed way. So I remain silent. There is no point answering silly questions. When at last I fall into bed, I am exhausted and also worried about everything I have heard. I cannot help thinking that no one cares about the truth or how we really lived during the last five years and also that the less I say about Ireland the better. No one will ever understand the loneliness of Clonea Strand or what it was like to be an alien.

ONCE AGAIN I WAKE UP LATE. Madame La Bruyère is in my room holding a pair of boy's brown trousers in a soft woolen material. She tells me that my father has asked her to find me something that I can wear to ride in. I try them on and they fit my waist; she will cut them below the knee and sew on two buttons. She has also found a pair of thick woolen socks that come right up to my knees. I have two woolen sweaters, my real leather shoes from Ireland and Blanche Dawnay's belt. I am blissfully happy to be

Mimi with her mother, Madame La Bruyère, and Mabel Smith.

Me out hunting a few years later.

home. From now on I will have breakfast at eight with my father in his room and at ten I'll meet him at the stables and we will ride together. Tommy is too small for me now; his work is pulling the pony trap in the afternoon. Instead, I ride Clotaire, a lazy old thoroughbred who never won a race.

After a while I become quite good again at recognizing crops and the size of fields. As always my father talks to several farmers and everyone he meets. One morning he introduces me to Simon Delangle, saying "This brave man always accompanied your mother on her visits to your aunt Lillie in Touraine. It was dangerous because they had to cross the frontier between occupied and unoccupied France without being noticed by the Germans. However, I always felt that she was safe with him because he is from that part of the country. He knew how to find out exactly when to cross his father's farm by way of a secret signal: when the curtains in a window on the top floor were drawn shut, it meant danger. He is a brave and reliable man."

On our way home, my father often whistles old hunting tunes, among them *"Le chevreuil de Bourgogne"*—the roebuck from Burgundy. I remember it and whistle it with him. "I see that you haven't forgotten how to ride and I am glad to hear that you haven't forgotten how to whistle." I smile at him as we ride along together and ask: "Would you like to hear some Irish tunes?"

"Yes, please." So I whistle for him "The Mountains of Mourne" and "The Rose of Tralee," and then one with a livelier tempo.

"What is the last one called?"

"It's called 'The Walls of Limerick.' It's also a dance, and I can dance it!" He looks at me astonished. "Where did you learn how to dance?"

"In the Technical School during recreation."

"Whistle 'The Walls of Limerick' again for me."

He joins in and I realize that he has a very good ear for music. After we get back to the stables and see our horses happily into their stalls, we walk slowly toward the house for lunch, stopping on the bridge. Leaning against the green railing, he asks me to show him how I dance.

"Yes, but you must whistle; I can't dance and whistle at the same time." He starts to whistle "The Walls of Limerick."

"No, the tune is right but the tempo is much too slow—try again faster, faster . . ." From the middle of the bridge, standing very straight and still, I look at him, pause a moment, and then fling back my head and start to dance as well as I can, not missing a single step or a beat, with a serious face. I dance until the tune is over, then give him a deep and serious bow. He smiles with astonishment and pleasure, and I must admit that I am quite pleased with myself! I love to dance!

The following morning my parents leave for Paris, where my father has business to attend to concerning the horses. That afternoon I am reading in the library when I hear terrible screams. I run to the stables, where I find two men firmly holding Marguerite Tessier by her arms. She is screaming and screaming in front of her house, like a madwoman. Two other men are holding a very thin and wrinkled little old man who is so weak he can barely stand up. It turns out he is a repatriated prisoner of war. He is Marguerite Tessier's husband, Marcel, but she doesn't recognize him because he has changed so much and she absolutely does not want him in her house and in her bed.

There must be a mistake, she cries. This is not the man she married; she does not want him. She is told that there is no mistake; she must be reasonable and control herself.

As I watch I can well understand poor Marguerite's shock and feelings. Adults also forget the faces of their loved ones. I feel very sad, too, for the miserable-looking Marcel, rejected after five years in a prison camp. Perhaps when he gets stronger and can ride again he will start to feel better? Before the war he was a jockey, and that is how he came to work and ride horses at Le Mesnil.

Mabel sees me standing alone. She comes to me and takes my hand as if I were a child and together we walk

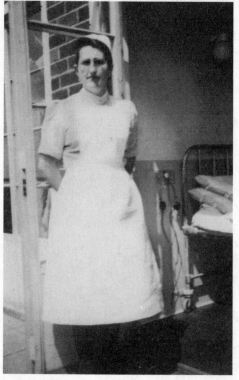

Marcel Tessier several years after having been a prisoner of war in Germany. Margaret Smith at Standish House Sanatorium, where she nursed men and women from the armed forces from 1945 to 1947.

back to the house. She says that the war has made many victims. At last I ask her where her younger daughter Gladys is. Tears run down her face, and she does not answer. I don't understand, because her elder daughter Margaret is working as a nurse in England and will only come back in 1947. Her son Robert is now at Le Mesnil and her husband George has come back safely from a prison camp near Paris where he spent the war with other mostly elderly English citizens. But Gladys, who is only a year older than I, is not here. Now I am very worried that something awful has happened to her.

Once in the house I look for my sister. She is sitting by herself in the drawing room. She doesn't have a book; she is staring out of the window with a worried expression, doing nothing, just waiting for our parents to return. Except at mealtimes she sits like this every morning and afternoon. I am really worried about her. Is she just lazy or is she ill? I try to make her talk to me without much success and I don't know what to do. Perhaps she is terrified that our parents will not return?

There was a telephone call this morning: Erasme de Contades-Gizeux, aged twenty, the only son of my parents' friends and the brother of my friends Guyonne, Alix and Renée, was killed in a battle near Colmar. He was in a tank of the 2nd Armored Division commanded by the French general Leclerc de Hautecloque. Later we heard that the tank he was in received a direct hit and went up in flames. When his coffin was sent home, it was very small, the size of a shoe box. At his funeral I felt that I was going to faint.

March 3rd in my diary: While our parents are in Paris and Chantilly on horse-related business, we have quiet meals with Madame de Cazotte and the two secretaries, Mademoiselle Chauvel and Madame Bodin. One day after lunch, I curl up in a deep armchair in the round library and read a French book by Balzac. I have not been there long when André comes and asks me if I'd like to walk the dogs with him. I'm happy to get some exercise and agree to meet him at the stables in ten minutes. He arrives with Mickey,

Mummy's dachshund, and Smack, Daddy's spaniel, who follows happily wagging his tail. We go to a small kennel to get Rip, André's greyhound. André is wearing a large brown coat with deep pockets. In silence, with the three dogs at his heels, we start walking. They all seem to know exactly where they are going and what they are about. Quietly I follow and soon we are in the woods. André and the dogs begin to slow down, and then, next to a hedge, they stop. When André makes a small sign with his hand, Mickey and Smack jump into the hedge and a rabbit jumps out. Then Rip moves into action, jumping onto the rabbit and breaking his neck. André picks up the rabbit and carefully presses its stomach with his thumbs to make him pee, then puts the rabbit into one of his deep pockets. We continue our walk for just a few yards and once again André signals to the dogs. Within seconds we have another rabbit. "That will do," he says quietly and we start to walk again at a faster pace until we come to some brambles.

Carefully he parts them with a stick and makes a sign to me to come and look. It is a snare, but there is nothing in it. We walked on and he checks two other snares, which are also empty. We turn around and walk back to the stables. Rip is put back in his kennel and we walk back to the house with the other dogs, entering through the kitchen door. No one is around. André goes straight into the larder room and he puts the two rabbits on a table. A short while later the cook will gut and skin them.

"You don't talk much," he says.

"No," I answer.

"Neither do I, better like that . . . must get back to my work."

He goes back to his work and I to my book. I understand now why we eat rabbit every day.

From then on I often "walk the dogs" after lunch with André. He has given me another reason to be happy to be home again. We always come back from our walks with the exact number of rabbits that are necessary to feed everyone in our house including our guests, neighbors who need them and the home for the elderly in our village.

The following day I receive a long letter from Mai, with all the Dungarvan news. There is also a letter from Wally, who is very bitter because she didn't come home with us. She is bored living with her sister. Her letter has something unreal about it, and only when I have read it a second time do I understand what it is: the letter ends with "lots of love and kisses." I laugh, but I answer both letters that morning before riding by myself on Clotaire. The weather has become warmer and many large yellow butterflies have appeared. The reality of home is sinking in and I cannot help noticing sadly how many trees have disappeared for firewood.

IN THE AFTERNOON I GO AGAIN and visit Jackie and Margarita for tea and I see my little cousins. Margarita lets me give Jacques-Marie his bottle. I've never held such a tiny baby in my arms before. It is strangely moving and I make a silent wish that one day I will have a warm and affectionate family like theirs. They begin to tell me about the war in France, and how our various cousins and friends lived and fought.

Myriam spent the whole war, except for school holidays, in a convent boarding school called "Les Oiseaux" in Moulins. She is well and extremely pretty. Her brothers were both in active service, Pierre with the Spahis in Morocco.

As to our Raoul-Duval uncles: Claude, a flight lieutenant in the Western desert, was a Commandeur de la Légion d'Honneur, and Gerry had fought valiantly at Bir Hakeim and been awarded the Croix de Guerre and la Légion d'Honneur. Our Decazes cousins, Jacques and Edouard, had also been decorated, with the Croix de Guerre and the Croix du Combattant Volontaire, respectively.

Cousin Louis was twenty when the war started. He was an Aspirant de Cavalerie-Cadet officer who participated in one of the last French military charges on horseback against German cannons. He was wounded in the knee and taken prisoner near a small Alsatian village where an SS regiment was preparing a banquet to celebrate their victory. Someone got a message to them that a young French man had a bullet in his knee and that he would surely lose his leg and perhaps his life if it was not extracted at once. An SS surgeon agreed to do the job. Five men had to hold Louis on a kitchen table while the doctor extracted the bullet without anesthetic. After the operation, the SS doctor returned to his banquet and Louis's life was saved. He was sent as a prisoner of war to work on a farm in Rhénanie until 1942, when he came back to France. Louis then joined the French Resistance in the Morvan, where at the time of the Liberation he saved the lives of several young German soldiers taken prisoner and about to be shot. In September 1944, he left for China with the Sainteny Mission. He is now a captain, still in China, and I am longing to meet him.

Our cousin Rose's brother, Pierre de Bellet, was also in Germany. He is now back in France but in a sanatorium. He has tuberculosis in both lungs and he is very ill. I ask Madame Bodin to send him my monthly chocolate ration. I'm not being heroic—I just don't like sweets. Aunt Maimaine is doing her best to have him sent to Switzerland where he will get better care and she will look after him financially.

On March 6 we all go to have lunch at Juigné. I am told to wear my best skirt and jumper and I am thrilled at the idea of seeing my childhood friends, Jacques-Henri, François and their little sister Marie. We leave at nine in the morning and first stop at Malicorne to say "Bonjour" to the Marquise de Vesins, a very old and charming woman who loves music. We don't stay long, as we don't want to be late for lunch and Madame de Cazotte is very anxious to see her sons Jacques and Denis. We drive slowly up the avenue and I recognize the château. The whole family comes

Flight Lieutenant Claude Raoul-Duval on standby in the Western desert, 1942. Commandeur de la Légion d'Honneur, Companion de la Libération, DFC.

Uncle Gerry Raoul-Duval at Bir Hakeim, where his bravery earned him the Ordre de la Division with the Croix de Guerre and a citation for bravery from General de Gaulle.

My cousins, Louis de Lesseps, Aspirant de Cavalerie; Edouard Decazes, who served with the 27th Battaillon de Chasseurs Alpin and was decorated with the Croix du Combattant Volontaire, 1939–1945; and Jacques Decazes, who served with the 183rd Régiment d'Artillerie, was cited with the Ordre du Régiment on June 29, 1940 and decorated with the Croix de Guerre, 1939–1945.

out to greet us as we get out of the car. I find that Jacques-Henri has grown a lot and so has François, who now wears spectacles. I don't recognize Marie, but their parents and grandparents look very much as I remembered them. We meet the Cazotte boys and also Stani de Clermont-Tonnerre, who is staying with his cousins because his family's château in Normandy was destroyed during a battle.

We have lunch in a large dining room, its walls hung with four of the most beautiful tapestries I have ever seen. They represent the four elements, earth, air, fire and water. We are asked the usual stupid questions and I try to answer as clearly as possible. The adults tell us a lot of things about Ireland as visualized through books or the eyes of their Irish governesses. Because I had not gone to school I didn't know about the historical ties between France and Ireland and the great friendship that existed between the two countries.

Jacques-Henri de Durfort remembers particularly vividly how in 1940 in a caravan of cars that also included my parents and a stallion, they left for their property, Le Bois-Rouaud, south of the Loire. It was there that they would bury both their family silver and ours under a toolshed in the vegetable garden, where it safely remained until the war was over. The Marquis and Marquise de Juigné, his grandparents, remained calmly behind awaiting the arrival of the Germans. Both the Durfort, whose family title is duc de Lorge, and the Juigné are ancient French nobility. Then aged eleven, Jacques-Henri was very frightened. He was allowed to take with him one treasured possession. He chose his goldfish, which he felt he really could not abandon to the enemy. He traveled in his mother's car for fourteen hours holding the fishbowl full of water firmly between his knees. A few weeks later, they all returned when the battle was lost and the area occupied. For part of the war, the Château de Juigné was taken over by the Germans. Our parents returned to Le Mesnil, where no major damage had been done.

After lunch we all go and sit in the large staircase hall

and watch a very amusing "comédie" that the boys have prepared to celebrate our return. It is a play written by Eugene Labiche called *L'Affaire de la rue de Lourcine*. The boys play all the roles, and Denis and Stani are the best actors, though all are very funny in the old-fashioned clothes they wear as costumes. Afterwards we go for a walk in the park and the boys take lots of photographs. Jacques-Henri asks me how we survived and I start to tell him, but soon we are called—it's time to go home. Later I seldom spoke about the war or about our life in Ireland. It was too complicated and anyway it was impossible to compare one experience to another. I tried to forget and yet I knew that I would be haunted by it all my life.

All along the road back to Le Mesnil we see many army vehicles, ambulances, tanks, machine guns, and trucks with "U.S." written on them. The war is not yet over. There are still fierce battles in eastern France and pockets of German resistance near the ports of St. Nazaire, La Rochelle and Royan. It is nearly dark, and we are all talking and laughing in the car after our happy day at Juigné.

As we stop in front of the steps of Le Mesnil, André comes out to open the doors of the car and I get a glimpse of his devastated face. Something awful must have happened . . . he goes straight to my father and they disappear together. At dinner, I hear that Gladys, the daughter of George the groom and Mabel his wife, is dead and so is her baby. I am horrified. She is only a year older than I. She died in terrible agony, as neither chloroform nor antibiotics were given to women having babies in Parisian hospitals.

"We must not talk about it, she was a bad girl, she had an American friend, yes! She made a lot of trouble, she was a bad girl . . . Of course it is very sad for her parents, but . . ." is all that I hear. I am horrified by the cold, matter-of-fact cruelty of adults and I know that at the age of eighteen she could not have been bad to the point of deserving such a death and the death of her child. I can't eat anything at dinner, and afterward do not go to the drawing room. Instead, I go right to bed, where I cry myself to sleep.

Stani de Clermont-Tonnerre, Jacques de
Cazotte, Denis de Cazotte, François de
Durfort, and Jacques-Henri de Durfort
in costume at Juigné, 1945.

First Lieutenant Jay McEvoy, U.S. Army, at
the large American base near Le Mesnil,
1944.

My cousin Hubert Maurice Fauquet-
Lemaître, a Cadet de Saumur, wounded
and made prisoner at the battle of Saumur,
June 19, 1940. Decorated with la Croix
de Guerre and Légion d'Honneur,
1939–1945.

The next morning I go to Mabel's cottage. She is all alone and ignored, sitting by the table, staring into space. I give her a kiss and sit beside her in silence. Soon, I realize that she does not know I am there, or perhaps does not really want me. She wants to be alone with the memory of her beautiful Gladys and her tiny baby. As I walk home, I think of my friend. I know that she was not bad, she was young and pretty, she and her baby are two more victims of this ghastly war. That night I have my nightmare. I am riding a great gray wave . . . Help! Help! I am drowning.

THERE IS A LARGE U.S. CAMP near us and as was their habit my parents have invited six young American officers for dinner. One general comes regularly and talks about the war in detail. He became a good friend of my father's and we are kept very well informed. They do this once a week, and some officers come several times, others only once. One who comes often is Lieutenant Jay McEvoy. He is a great favorite of Mummy's because he comes from San Francisco. He usually brings his friend Lieutenant Harold Parsons from Boston, and I have a drawing of them both in my autograph book. They always come with presents, such as chocolates, cigarettes and chewing gum. I accept everything and redistribute afterward. No one ever seems to want the chewing gum. Mummy manages to get letters to San Francisco faster, thanks to Jay. We all feel so grateful to the Americans for helping to liberate France, and the very least we can do is to have them regularly for meals, since they are all very homesick and some are shell-shocked. They don't seem to mind always eating rabbit—in fact, most of them think they are eating French chicken. We do not explain.

One evening at dinner, however, there was a small diplomatic incident of sorts because the main dish was a delicious ox tongue, sliced and surrounded with various vegetables. An American officer asked what they were about to eat and when my father told them, their faces turned green; they shook their heads and said that they were very sorry but they could not eat anything out of an animal's mouth. It was just not done in America. Our problem now was that there was nothing else in the kitchen that we could give them instead, as meat was still strictly rationed. My mother suggested eggs, and they responded enthusiastically, that yes please they would love some eggs. A few minutes later boiled eggs appeared from the kitchen and were being passed around. Then my father said in a low and solemn voice, in French, "You see how strange some men are. They won't eat something that comes out of an animal's mouth, but they are quite happy to eat something that comes out of its arse." My mother looked quite shocked and I had great difficulty not laughing.

There is an important meeting being held at Yalta between Churchill, Roosevelt and Stalin. Roosevelt is seriously ill and will be dead in a couple of weeks, Churchill has pneumonia, and only Stalin is fighting fit. General de Gaulle has not been invited and the resulting agreements prove to be a disaster for half of Europe.

Sometimes the Americans take us for rides in their jeeps, which is strictly forbidden but great fun. Many signed my autograph book: James E. Kelly, Abilene Texas; Van Kilzek, Escarabu Av., Chicago; Lieutenant Milo Goldenberg, Wisconsin; Isaac T. Reynolds, Wilmington, North Carolina. Americans never stop smiling, and I suppose it is their way of being polite. Perhaps it is because she is a Californian that Madame de Cazotte smiles all the time, and yet her smile does not hide the tragedy written on her face. Her husband is in Koenigstein, a prison fortress for officers in Bohemia. She is terribly worried about him and also about the future of her two sons, although at the moment they are safe with the Durfort family at Juigné. There is perhaps also another reason. She is already feeling ill and possibly has a premonition that soon she will die of cancer. I can see how vulnerable she is and feel deeply sorry for her.

The following day we all went in the car to Paris.

Mummy wants to take us to the dentist and I ask her if she can also take me to the oculist. I have always been a little shortsighted but now I am worried because my eyes are very weak. I often see small black spots and I have trouble reading. Also, my handwriting in my diary has become very strange, all pointed and jerky and aggressive, but I do not mention this. This arose as a result of stress and depression that many adolescents and children suffered from and was totally ignored by adults.

The next morning we go to the dentist. Miraculously my teeth are perfect, but Marguerite obligingly needs a little work done. In the afternoon and on the following day, we visit Uncle François and Aunt Zette de Bellet, Uncle Jean and Aunt Tess de Boislisle, Tante Edith and my cousin Myriam de Lesseps. It is lovely to see them all and rather boring having to answer many of the same questions.

I also meet a brilliant girl, Janine Lambling, who is a little older than I am and the daughter of friends of Mummy who are both doctors. She is studying science and is very interested in politics and communism. If I swear not to tell anyone, she will take me to a meeting the next time I am in Paris, and I agree to go.

We do not have time for the oculist, but as I often have colds, Mummy has decided to have my tonsils taken out. My throat hurts terribly, the anesthetic did not work or the doctor did not use enough. I feel battered inside and out.

While we are in Paris, Uncle Richard arrives at the flat. We are thrilled to meet him and I think that he is absolutely wonderful. We also meet Lieutenant Colonel Diggle, who is the commander of all the British military police in Paris and an impressive man.

In the very early morning, I get up and go for long walks alone along the banks of the Seine. I am under the spell of the beauty of Paris: the buildings, the monuments, and the pink and white chestnut trees in flower along the riverbanks. Perhaps one day a young man will put his arm around my waist and we will walk here together. For the moment I am madly in love with the beauty of Paris and my

My mother with her
brother Richard at
Le Mesnil.

Marguerite, François de
Kergolay and me at Le
Mesnil, 1945.

eyes drink in the mother-of-pearl sky over Notre Dame, a shade of all the nuances of the color gray.

When we return home, we meet our new teacher, Mademoiselle Sousgniac, who will stay at Le Mesnil for a few months and give us lessons. She is twenty years old and her parents are very short of money. I gather that this is the main reason she was chosen and I don't know who found her. She has never taught before and her lessons are not inspiring. She gives me a lot of grammar to learn and suggests I read some French books, which I am doing already. I don't know what or when she teaches Marguerite.

On the other hand, Monsieur Biot, my piano teacher, is wonderful and inspiring. He is an elderly man with a hunchback, a beautiful head and luminous eyes. He is a great musician and with him I discover Debussy, Ravel and Olivier Messiaen. He is also the organist at the cathedral in Le Mans and invites me to listen to him at eleven o'clock mass the following Sunday. I accept and bicycle into Le Mans, climb the steepest stairs I have ever been up and sit beside him while he plays celestial Gregorian music. It is there, listening to the organ and admiring the lovely twelfth- and thirteenth-century Gothic architecture of the cathedral, that for the first time, I understand a little the meaning of spirituality.

I will return to the cathedral on many other Sundays. I also go regularly to my weekly music lessons on my bicycle. It is just a little farther than from Clonea Strand to Dungarvan. My father has bought me a secondhand piano. It is tucked away in a tower so that no one can hear me practicing scales and be driven berserk with my determination to become a musician. Earlier, I had practiced on the beautiful grand piano in the drawing room.

Our closest neighbors, Aymard and Amicie de Nicolay, came for lunch. They live at Montfort le Rotrou. They are warmhearted and charming. They have four children and speak English, which is nice for Marguerite.

My diary reads that I receive a letter from Blanche Dawnay and one from Wally with the usual complaints, and a very nice two-page letter from Mick Connors giving me all the Dungarvan news. As I don't have a photograph of him, I draw a little portrait sketch in my diary, carefully drawing a rather long lock of hair over his forehead and left eye. I am pleased because it is a pretty good likeness. When my parents return, I show them his letter. They are both shocked and surprised that a young man should bother to write to me.

The following Saturday, Madame de Laveaucoupet gives a small dance party in Le Mans for her children. I am invited and am very happy because I make some charming new friends. I like Diane very much and also her brothers François and Guy. I also meet Nicole d'Argenlieu and her sisters. We dance swings, waltzes and tangos from five-thirty in the evening to six o'clock in the morning. Twenty boys and twenty girls, we all drink champagne and have an excellent supper and then breakfast.

Uncle Pierre Fauquet-Lemaître has arrived with his wife and daughter. Nicole is a dear little girl who looks like Alice in Wonderland. Uncle Pierre fought as an aviator in both World Wars and his son Maurice was wounded during the battle of Saumur. They will stay a week.

*F*OR THE EASTER HOLIDAYS Le Mesnil is going to be filled with people. There is of course Madame de Cazotte. Madame de Redon, whose husband was killed in 1940, is coming with her four children, three girls and a boy. We are also going to have Johnny and Bertie de Flers, thirteen-year-old twins whose brave parents are still in concentration camps, as they were very active in the Resistance and saved many lives. I am greatly looking forward to meeting the twins.

They all arrive by train. The Redon family is typically French; they have very pointed noses, and Madame de Redon is dressed all in black. My immediate favorites are the twins. Soon I think of them as younger brothers. They have two sisters, Beatrice and Marie-Claire, who are our age but are not coming, as they have gone separately to other people for their holidays. I think that they must hate not being together at such a dramatic time, since they are already separated from their father and mother, of whom they have had no news.

As we all sit around the large oval table, I can see that the Redon children do not like us. They all call my father Uncle Jean and my mother Aunt Elisabeth and yet they are not our cousins. I recalled that I had seen this scene before in a nightmare in Ireland and it makes me shiver.

"Our parents were lucky," I think. "They had the company of other people's children."

The advantage of not being able to speak a language fluently is that it gives one time to be more observant, to study faces and listen more carefully. It is astonishing to hear all the half-truths, the futile lies. I notice that people who speak a great deal seldom think before they speak and only very rarely listen to others.

At the end of the holidays, the Redon family returns to Paris. We are all hoping that the war will soon be over. There is still heavy fighting on the Rhine and elsewhere in Germany. Trains of prisoners of war keep arriving in every major town. Johnny and Bertie, who speak perfect English, do not go back to their school in Paris. They are to stay longer at Le Mesnil and I wonder why. A few days later I am sitting with a book near the house when I see Johnny running towards the garden. I run after him and find him collapsed on a bench by the tennis court. My father has just told him and his brother that their father has died but that their mother is alive and that she will arrive at Le Mesnil in a few days' time.

I hold Johnny in my arms and I think that his sobs will never end. Nothing can stop his crying, no words can console him, his little boy's heart is broken. After a long time, we slip back into the house through the kitchen door. I take Johnny up to his room, take off his shoes and jacket, and put him in bed, covering his shaking body with a blanket. I pull the curtains and he is still crying as he falls asleep.

Then I go and look for poor little Bertie, who is nowhere to be found. I tell my father and everyone starts searching for him but to no avail. My mother, Madame de Cazotte and Marguerite have gone to the hairdressers for the afternoon. Someone says not to worry; that he will turn up when he gets hungry, and that person is right. Bertie appears the next day at lunch time, but he is no longer the same boy. He doesn't speak; he doesn't cry; he is in shock and has gone completely numb from panic and pain. I think that all my sadness is little compared to theirs. Their father is dead; at least mine is alive and understands me.

Madame de Flers arrives from Ravensbruck a few days later. She is tall, well over five feet, but weighs less than ninety pounds. Never have I seen anyone so thin, so completely bald, with large, lifeless sunken eyes. She eats a tiny amount of food in her room and speaks only in a whisper. If the weather is warm she is taken into the garden by the round central pond with its goldfish and waterlilies, and there she sits immobile in an armchair. Bertie sits on a chair in silence beside her. She wants no one else. She does not ask for her daughters or for Johnny, so he and I sit on the tennis court bench in the distance watching them, and holding each other's hand. After a while Johnny whispers to me, "She doesn't want me—she doesn't love me anymore."

"She is very ill—see how thin she is? She isn't strong enough yet to love you all at once—she can only get used again to one of you at a time. She will love you when she gets better . . ."

"Will she die?"

"I don't think so—everyone is looking after her . . ."

"But she doesn't want me . . ."

"My mother doesn't want me either."

"Why? She always had enough to eat?"

"She wanted a son, so I disappointed her. Now I have grown too much. When she left us in Ireland, I was only a child. I'm now grown up in many ways—I think, I see, I listen . . . My mother is much happier with Marguerite who has gone back into babyland and is practically sucking her thumb again to please her . . . Come Johnny, let's leave this sad garden. We can go for a walk by the river. We'll look after each other and try our best to manage without mothers."

A few days later, Madame de Flers asked to be taken to Paris. She left early one morning with her sons. She slowly recovered, yet never completely. Out of her four children, she loved only one. Her eldest daughter, Béatrice, was so traumatized that she committed suicide.

At the age of twenty, on the afternoon of my father's funeral, I very nearly did the same. I went to his room; it was dark, the shutters were closed. I locked the door and sat at his table by the window. Slowly I opened the secret drawer and took out his revolver. I put a bullet in and snapped it shut. I put the barrel in my mouth and felt the cold steel between my teeth, "One—two—three . . ." I quickly put the revolver back on the table. Three rhymed with Louis. I had a two-month-old baby, Jean-Louis. I couldn't die. I had to live—my duty was to live. I could never abandon my little boy.

The following week, Comte François de Lubersac, a friend of my parents, arrives from an officers' prison camp, Zeust Oflag 6A, where he has spent five years. He isn't in quite as bad condition as Madame de Flers, although he too is terribly thin. After a while he even can tell us funny stories about his prison and how much they all suffered from the millions of fleas and how, when they were nearly starving, they ate roast mice. He is a brave and charming man.

I know that we children of the war will never recover. We will always be different. People won't understand us, because our aims are unclear, our actions unpredictable, our codes of honor and our friendships unconventional. We will become the adults of shattered childhoods with deep invisible scars. As we seldom speak about our feelings, adults quickly ignore us, saying "They are young, they will forget. . . ," and they go about their usual business and pleasures. Children suffer differently. Unlike adults, they do not understand the reasons for wars and no one really explains. They don't participate in heroic actions or great adventures, and they don't have the consolations of love affairs a thousand times more exciting and passionate than those in peacetime. They, poor little devils, are always alone and frightened in their cold and narrow beds.

If I have children one day, I swear that I will never part with them in wartime. It is a thousand times better to suffer together. Returning home after so much hope and so many dreams is also painful. One can never forget having been abandoned, even if it was for our safety, and our parents, particularly my mother, who had not seen us grow up, insisted on treating us as if we were still eight and twelve years old. No, I swear, if I ever have children I will never part with them in wartime.

ON THE 30TH OF APRIL, the Russians enter Berlin. Hitler and his gang commit suicide. On the 7th of May we hear on the radio that the war has ended and that victory will be formally announced tomorrow. At exactly three o'clock the church bells all over France will ring together. Our dead will not have been sacrificed in vain. We will be eternally grateful to them, for they have given us back peace and freedom. I think of our many military prisoners of war who are still in Germany and also of the horrific concentration camps where so many men, women and children are still waiting to be liberated. I pray that they will soon come home.

I am so happy this evening that I kiss and hug François de Lubersac. He doesn't seem surprised, and he kisses me right back. The world has gone mad, but this time mad with joy.

The next day—Victory Day—I go to early mass at Savigné to thank God. We have lunch as usual at twelve thirty, and at exactly three, we all go out of the house and stand together on the front steps to listen to the church bells. The bell of Le Mesnil, normally used to call us for meals, is ringing loudly. I notice that my father is looking very annoyed.

"What is the matter?" I ask him.

"Are you deaf?" he says. "Listen carefully—the bells of our church in Savigné aren't ringing." I listen more attentively. He is right. I can hear the bells of St. Corneille, of Fatines, of Yvré-l'Evêque but nothing from Savigné. My father tells André to take his bicycle and go to the presbytery at once to see "what the devil Monsieur le Curé is doing," and says that if our bells are not ringing soon my father will be over there himself. Ten minutes later all our bells are ringing loudly and André comes back quite out of breath from his hasty ride.

"What was the problem?" asked my father.

"There was no problem at all, Monsieur Jean, only Monsieur le Curé had not finished his lunch."

"Holy cow," I say under my breath, and start to laugh.

After listening to the bells, we gather in the drawing room around the radio and listen for a long time to the historic world broadcasts. In the late afternoon we go to the Savigné cemetery with all the people of our village to pray for all who have died. We sing together the Te Deum, then the brass band plays the "Marseillaise" and the national anthems of all our Allies.

We have dinner as usual at eight and I go to bed at ten, totally exhausted from emotion. At two in the morning, we are all awakened by the brass band of our village, composed of twenty-three musicians, all either very young or very old men. They play a large variety of well-polished instruments—bugles, clarinets, trumpets, horns, bassoons and drums. They are in great spirits and are leading the way around our house playing a cheerful military march called "Sambre et Meuse," the names of two rivers in eastern France where battles were fought between the French and the Germans. They are followed by well over three hundred men, women, and children, some of whom are carrying lanterns, who have come to celebrate with us in this spontaneous way the end of the war.

Quickly we all dress and run downstairs and out into the dark night to join the merry crowd. My father tells André to go to the cellar and bring up bottles of wine. André has no trouble finding several men to help him while Mabel and Solange get all the glasses they can find. When the music stops, it is replaced by the glorious symphony of popping corks and general merriment. I keep busy filling glasses. Everyone seems to be talking at once, all slightly drunk from a mixture of excitement, relief, wine and happiness. When the musicians begin the farandole from *Carmen* by Georges Bizet, we begin to dance, catching the nearest available hand—a boy, a girl, a man, an elderly woman, a little child. Soon we are all dancing gracefully, holding hands high above our heads, around Le Mesnil and it is only then as I dance and sing "L'Amour est enfant de Bohême"—"Love is a Bohemian child, who never never obeys the law, and if I love you and you love me, well then, look out, look out for thee". . . In the dark moonless night, so many happy people all holding each other's hands, I realize that at last the war in Europe is over.

Me continuing in the family tradition with Bison Futé, winner at Auteuil in 1981, with Mr. Ashley Chanler, and in the background his daughter, Mafalda Stenbock-Fermor, and my friend Geneviève du Breil.

Miss Walsh

Wally came back to Le Mesnil in June 1945. Until that date, because the war in Europe was just over, very little traveling was allowed for ordinary civilians. We were all happy to see her again and she was assured by my parents that she could live with us and be looked after financially until the end of her life. She was given a comfortable room, was received with great warmth and treated like a heroine. Her only occupation consisted of being a companion for Marguerite. Solange, the little house maid, made her bed and kept her room tidy. I also knew that she had been given a comfortable sum of money but I was not told the amount.

After a few weeks I noticed that Wally was not happy at Le Mesnil. She spoke only a few words of French and she was no longer in command, no longer "The Boss" as she had been in Ireland. She also made clear that she thought that both my sister and I had become too independent, and that in fact I "had gone to the dogs," as I now drank a little red wine at meals. Several times in private she gave me hell, saying that I would "end in the gutter." Her screams and tears were frightening and not those of a normal, well-balanced adult. American officers still came once a week for dinner and she always made me beg for cigarettes for her (French cigarettes were rationed) and she would be very cross with me if I did not succeed in getting any.

In November 1945 my Father decided that he had to go to America. He wanted to see Mr. Widener in Philadelphia about his horses, which my Father had saved from the Germans and remained at Le Mesnil. At the risk of his own life my Father made out false papers transferring ownership. The valuable horses were relatively safe as long as they were owned by a French citizen but subject to immediate confiscation if owned by foreigners or by disenfranchised Jews. He did the same for Lord Derby's horses and asked his friend the Marquis de Saint Sauveur to do the same for the horses of Monsieur Jean Stern—because he, being Jewish, would also have had his horses stolen by the Germans. My Father decided to take my Mother, my sister and me with him, travel to New York on a ship called *The America* and then continue on to California to visit our relatives there. This journey for business and family reasons was going to be very expensive and the houses of our American cousins were not large. My Father told Wally that he would pay for her journey to Ireland and give her some extra money so that she could stay with her sister Madge until our return in January, when she could return to Le Mesnil. He was going to close our house while we were away.

Wally was absolutely furious with Father. She said that she had always wanted to visit the United States, that we had treated her badly and that she would never forgive any of us. She returned to live with her sister Madge and refused ever to come back to France. She continued to receive regular financial help. From 1960 until her death in 1979, she lived in a comfortable home for elderly people called Woodlock near the town of Portlaw in County Waterford.

In 1961 my Mother had a horse called Right Royal that won the French Derby. Wally heard about it and wrote to my mother asking for a very large sum of money. None too pleased about the amount, my Mother nevertheless sent it to her. A few weeks later she received a thank you note that read, "Thank you for the money you sent me, I have given it to the nuns of Woodlock so that after my death they will pray for my soul." This time my mother was really furious, as she was quite religious herself and thought that Wally could have at least included my Mother's soul as well in the good nuns' prayers!

Personally, I could not help laughing. We never saw Wally again after she left France but we wrote to her, and sent her money, for the rest of her life. Many years later, after her death, I went to Woodlock to visit Winnie, Lady Waterford's younger sister. I asked to meet the Reverend Mother, who was absolutely charming. She remembered Miss Walsh, who had been both happy and very well liked at Woodlock.

Never Say Fail!

Keep pushing—'tis wiser
than sitting aside,
And dreaming and sighing
and waiting the tide.
In Life's earnest battle
They only prevail
Who daily march onward,
And never say fail!

With an eye ever open—
A tongue that's not dumb,
And a heart that will never
to sorrow succumb—
You'll battle and conquer
though thousands assail:
How strong and how mighty,
Who never say fail!

The spirit of angels
Is active I know
As higher and higher
In glory they go.
Me thinks on bright pinions
From heaven they sail,
To cheer and encourage
Who never say fail!

Ahead then keep pushing,
And elbow your way,
Unheeding the envious,
And asses that bray;
All obstacles vanish,
All enemies quail,
In the might of their wisdom
Who never say fail!

In life's rosy morning,
In manhood's firm pride,
Let this be the motto
Your footsteps to guide;
In storms and in sunshine,
Whatever assail—
We'll onward and conquer,
And never say fail!

One of my favorite poems, from the book *The Casket of Gems,* which often made me think of Winston Churchill's message never to despair, written by an anonymous American in the nineteenth century.

Acknowledgments

I WISH TO THANK and am most grateful to my following friends and cousins who most generously helped me with their advice, encouragement and photographs. Every contribution, without exception, was of great value, enabling me to build a picture of these war years and write the book:

Marina Aamodt, Agnes Albert, Veronica Ashbrooke, André Baeyens, Fernand Bartholoni, Patrick Beresford, Beatrice de Boisanger, Paul and Sue de Brantes, Philip Brutton, Jean Bulley, Andreas and Jane Buttimer, Mai Breen, Ariane Castaing, Denis de Cazotte, Hugh and Maria Ines Dawnay, Caroline Decazes, Antonia Devin, Peter and Sylvia Diggle, François and Ghislaine de Durfort, Jacques-Henri and Cecile de Durfort, Nicole Fauquet-Lemaître, Terry Fitzgerald, Mark Girouard, Rose Jackson, Teresa James, Mary Kaplan, Lee Katz, Jean-Michel and Térèse de Kermadec, Renée de Laffon, Beatrice Lambling, Anne-Marie Leroy, Jeanne de Lesseps, Edith Lewis, Karine McCall, Jay McEvoy, Peter Malone, Patricia Nix, Verne O'Hara, Polly Platt, Sylvia Raoul-Duval, Claude Raoul-Duval, Sally Scrope, Margaret Smith, Mafalda Stenböck Fermor, Norman Stokle, Nicole Stroh, Jane St. George, Elin Vanderlip and Tyrone and Caroline Waterford.

Special thanks to Patricia and Steven Hope, Patricia Oliver of The Hannon Press and to my editor at The Free Press, Chad Conway.